From Byfleet to the Bush

From Byfleet to the Bush
JACQUELINE PEARCE
An Autobiography

The Maids
Jean Genet

fantom
publishing

First published in 2012 by Fantom Films
fantomfilms.co.uk

Copyright © Jacqueline Pearce 2012

Jacqueline Pearce has asserted her moral right to be identified as the author of this work in accordance with the Copyright, Designs and Patents Act 1988.

All rights reserved.

A catalogue record for this book is available from the British Library.

Hardback Edition ISBN: 978-1-906263-86-7
Standard Paperback Edition ISBN: 978-1-906263-87-4

Typeset by Phil Reynolds Media Services, Leamington Spa
Printed and bound in the UK by ImprintDigital.com

Cover design by Dexter O'Neill

All photographs are from the author's personal collection; copyright holders are credited where known.

For my Father
Wherever you are Dad, I love you

Contents

Foreword by John Hurt — 1

Acknowledgements — 2

1: Byfleet — 5
2: The Convent Years — 25
3: Angie — 35
4: RADA — 45
5: Marriage and Movies — 55
6: Hollywood — 68
7: Ups and Downs — 80
8: Blake's 7 — 92
9: Aftermath — 105
10: Sanctuary — 117
11: Joel — 127
12: Cornwall — 139
13: London – Part One — 151
14: London – Part Two — 164
15: Africa — 172
16: Beating about the Bush — 185
17: A Bird in the Hand… — 195
18: Bush Baby — 207

Foreword

'Jackson', as I call her, is brave, capricious, wise and strangely foolish and gullible; on occasion prepared to take on mountainous odds and, almost in the same moment, fearful of a molehill. Her beauty has infected those on the peripheral but influential edges of her life; her personality is what has informed her friends.

In this candid account, her early family life, her professional life and indeed her private life are displayed always intriguingly, sometimes arrestingly and often movingly; and I shouldn't forget to say that her book is not short on wit or humour. She makes light of what most of us would find daunting and she is crippled by what many of us would take in our stride. She makes it clear that showbiz is not a life of glamour but of passion, many disappointments and a few dazzling pinnacles.

Best of all about this book, it is a heartfelt account of my friend's very real life.

John Hurt
February 2012

Acknowledgements

This book would never have been written without the help and encouragement of the following friends.

Dr Martin Rogerson who not only nagged me constantly when I was living in England but actually flew out to see me in Africa where he continued to enquire on a daily basis, 'How's the book coming along Jacks?' When he left eight days later he had managed to extract a promise from me that I would begin writing immediately. By then I would have agreed to *anything* just to get him off my back.

Martin also introduced me to my editor Douglas McNaughton who encouraged, supported, consoled and when necessary chivvied me along on the many occasions when I became convinced that I had bitten off far more than I could ever chew.

My web designer David Delfouneso who made me a present of my site on the condition that I write a blog. It was the response from readers that gave me the confidence to believe that with practice I might be able to write a book that people would want to read. My love and thanks to you all.

Daniel Grove and Sophie Clarke from the Vervet Monkey Foundation who every week schlepped to my cottage laden down with health-enhancing goodies from which Sophie would concoct delicious delicacies with which to tempt a capricious appetite. They always kept an eye on me. Thanks guys.

Bertus Kriel and Iwill Mashele who run PC Digital in Tzaneen Mall and who dealt kindly and patiently with my complete lack of IT skills and didn't turn a hair when I rushed in on a weekly basis sweating and hysterical, crying, 'My attachment won't send, help me, help me!' With the press of a button they would dispatch my latest chapter to Douglas and never reproached me once for my spectacular stupidity. Don't think you're free of me now guys, I shall be back...

My publisher Dexter O'Neill, who has to be one of the bravest men on the planet to agree to publish my small contribution to the world of letters. If I'm not banned before I'm published, I shall be amazed. Respect Dex, respect.

And Eleen Joubert who took over where Martin had left off, making repeated enquiries as to how the book was progressing. Eleen owns the Hill Top Country Lodge, a beautiful five-star guest house in Tzaneen. She is also an artist and her extraordinary talent has created an atmosphere that is truly magical. Times without number she has invited me to Hill Top, fed and watered (wined) me and tucked me into an enormous bed covered in antique linen in an enchanting room. I've yet to see a bill... Darling E, you're always there for me. Thank you.

And last but never least, my canine family and constant companions: Snooze, Toska and Rusty, who fill my life with love and laughter. And my mysterious, magical Africa. How I love you!

※

I am fully aware that there will probably be a large percentage of people who at some point, or indeed several, during the reading of this book will hurl it across the room shouting, 'FOR GOD'S SAKE WOMAN, GET A GRIP! PULL YOURSELF TOGETHER!' The point I have tried to make is that, for most of my life, I had no sense of 'self' and therefore there was nothing to pull and nowhere to grip.

I am also fully aware that my reactions to the situations in which I found myself were frequently neither admirable nor courageous. I don't doubt for a second that others with more courage, backbone and intelligence than I would have sailed through similar difficulties and emerged whole and triumphant many decades ago, before going on to make significant contributions to the world of their fellow man. Much as I would like to be among their number, I have to acknowledge that I'm not. Life's a bitch and I'm a wimp.

And yes, there are countless numbers of people whose suffering in appalling situations makes my own difficulties appear trivial and trite. All of this I accept and concur with. But no matter how inappropriate and over the top my reactions may be viewed as by others, I can only say that's how it was for me. Chronic depression is a state of despair due to the total absence of hope.

I know many people are cynical regarding the medical profession, but I can only feel immense gratitude for the huge help it has given me. I am particularly grateful for the tremendous advances in the understanding of, and treatment for, mental health issues. I can offer no better example than citing the fate of the Maid of Orleans, Saint Joan – a young girl who was burnt at the stake because she heard voices. These days she'd be on tablets…

1
Byfleet

I loved my life in Byfleet. No... I didn't. I loved Byfleet, not the life I lived there.

I was born in the (then) small town of Woking, Surrey on 20th December 1943 and, after her confinement, mother and child came home to Queens Avenue, Byfleet. In those days Byfleet was a small country village. Our fruit and vegetables were grown in the surrounding fields, harvested and delivered to the local greengrocers – two as I recall – to be purchased by the women of the village, carrying large, leather shopping bags or baskets of woven straw. Sheep and cattle grazed in gentle meadows, unaware of their imminent demise; they would appear later as legs, shoulders, saddles and offal in the window of our local butcher, the slaughterhouse being a few steps from the shop.

Our Avenue was lined with chestnut trees, so my parents, who were not known for their originality, named the house 'Chestnuts' and there I remained for the first seventeen years of my life. My mother didn't, but more about that later.

At the bottom of our garden was a large field, in the centre of which was a perfectly manicured, emerald green cricket pitch, where men dressed in pristine whites would play on drowsy Sunday afternoons. The other men of the village, replete with recently downed pints of beer at the Queens Head and the ritual Sunday lunch, lay heavily on striped canvas deckchairs as they formed a small group of spectators. Bees buzzed lazily in the warmth of the day, the wings of butterflies shimmered in the late afternoon sun, and mysterious shadows were cast by the leaves of oak trees as the gentle breeze parted their summer foliage and cajoled them into whispering their secrets. (If you think I'm seeing this through the rosy glow of nostalgia, where the birds always sang and the sun always shone, you're wrong; it frequently pissed down.)

The best thing from my point of view was not the cricket itself, but the tea we enjoyed afterwards in the wooden pavilion whose clock, centred in a protruding gable in the middle of its roof, would, at the appropriate time, signal the umpire to end the match so tea could commence. The wives of the players, all sporting aprons and hats, would prepare a feast of sausage rolls, cheese straws, cheese, tomato and Marmite sandwiches, egg and cress rolls, jam tarts, cup cakes, fancies, Battenburg cake and Swiss roll. Steaming amber liquid served from a dull silver cylinder flowed constantly into thick white cups, laced with milk and sugar, for the grown-ups; and there was Tizer, lemonade and ginger beer for the children.

I loved the cricket field; in summer it would be carpeted with celandines, buttercups, and daisies which I would weave into chains and place on my head and around my neck. Cow parsley grew in profusion from the ditch that ran around three sides of the field, the oak trees that had stood for centuries on its steep sides heavy with their summer foliage. All the houses on the left side of the Avenue had gardens with gates at the bottom that opened onto the field, enabling neighbours to chat together and children to play. Cowboys and Indians was a great favourite; but being the only girl in my peer group I was always the lone Indian, captured and bound to a tree, while Anthony Wand, Jeremy Bean and John Bragg fired *my* arrows at me. I still have a small scar in my right eyebrow, a reminder of the time when Ant got lucky. In order to gain admission into their gang, I had to squeeze a bunch of stinging nettles and not make any sound at all.

In the autumn, we played in the Avenue as the chestnut trees filled the street with russet-coloured leaves in which we could hide and roll around and fling great armfuls at each other, and shed huge, shiny conkers which we quickly threaded onto lengths of string, and had glorious conker fights. (Fuck you, Health and Safety.) We played marbles, jacks and hopscotch in the street (Queens Avenue being a cul-de-sac), swapped 'fag' cards as they were known then, and traded marbles. Jerry Bean, who lived next door, made intricate model aeroplanes out of balsa wood when he wasn't doing homework. His parents were both teachers at the secondary school in West Byfleet – his mother taught needlework, and his father was headmaster – so when it came to doing his homework, Jerry was between a rock and a hard place. Having passed his eleven plus he went to Woking Grammar School and eventually became a doctor.

At the open end of the Avenue was the main road leading to West Byfleet to the right and Old Byfleet to the left, which was bordered by a small wood containing an old house whose occupants rarely revealed themselves, and a very mysterious house at its far corner, 'Lake House'. Surrounded as it was by dank, stagnant water, with a canopy of trees bent with age and exhaustion excluding all light and defying the sun, it was frequently the subject of my childish imagination. Bulrushes grew around the edge of the lake; water lilies struggled to survive, the stench of dampness and decay filled the dense air, and I found myself irresistibly drawn to its shadowy interior. I was in thrall to its magic; even as a young child, I intuited the knowledge contained in darkness.

When I look back on my childhood, I am very aware of the comfort I received from nature, and the feel of the late 1940s and early fifties. There was only very occasional traffic in the village, although we did hit traffic jams when we returned from a hot Sunday spent on the beach at West Wittering. I can still recall the scents of clover, and huge red roses, their velvety petals heavy with morning dew; wild narcissi, bluebells and lily of the valley; the aroma of burning leaves and wood smoke as the melancholy of autumn hovered in the still air.

My favourite season was and remains winter. Jack Frost leaving intricate patterns on the inside of my bedroom window; sheets frozen on the washing line as dusk descended; snowmen, with coal noses and clay pipes between their arctic lips, whose jolly daytime demeanour became slightly sinister as night began to fall. More than anything I loved snow: its ability to transform all that was familiar into a fairytale world of magic, mystery and overwhelming beauty. Icicles hung from guttering, whose ugliness was concealed by the weight of whiteness that lay along its length and sparkled with jewel colours as it caught the sun. I exhaled white, frosty breath, imagining elegant holders containing forbidden cigarettes, and balls in ice palaces where all the guests wore white and dined from plates of silver and crystal.

I came home from school one December afternoon. It was dusk and had snowed heavily all day. I ran down the garden to the cricket field, pushed open the gate, and entered a magic world. A blood red sun was setting in a darkening sky; the bare branches of the trees, whose unclothed vulnerability touched my soul, were rimmed with silver frost; the cricket pavilion, now the palace of the 'Snow Queen'; and the snow before me still in its virgin state. I wanted to stay in that world of beauty forever. I raised my four-year-old arms to the setting sun, and ran towards it. I believed I could fly; that I was a part of all that surrounded me, protected me, and claimed me as its own. So all in all I had a great affection for bucolic Byfleet.

I loved sweets, and when rationing finally ended in the mid fifties I feasted on Rolos, Maltesers, Mars bars and Smarties. Prior to the end of rationing my father came home one night with a parcel of black-market butter and Mars bars, and despite gorging myself to the point of nausea, butter and Mars bars have remained lifelong pleasures. But what I loved most, and still do, was my bed. In the warmth of my horsehair mattress, covered by woollen blankets, I felt safe, secure and, above all, warm. Despite my passion for the beauty of winter, I hated being cold; I liked to view the winter landscape from the chair beside the fire in the sitting room (being from a lower-middle-class family, it was referred to as the 'lounge', a word I have come to loathe) before being turfed out by an adult. The fire was lit at four o'clock every afternoon; the only other heating in the house was provided by the boiler in the kitchen. It gave us hot water and, as central heating was unheard of in those days, meant that the kitchen was the only room in the house that was constantly warm.

In order to satisfy my passion for sweets, I stole money from my foster mother's purse. Every Saturday morning I was sent to do the shopping. As her own child remained in bed reading comics, I found the unfairness of the situation unacceptable and derived great pleasure from the half-crown I slipped into the pocket of my navy blue knickers. I also stole from the local sweetshop and will never forget the day when the owner, Mr Worsefold, suddenly appeared as I was making for the door, box of Maltesers in hand, and said, 'Would you mind putting those back please?' So great was my shame that I never stole from a shop again. But I continued to haunt the sweet shops in the village. Large glass jars containing lemonade powder (a great favourite), sticky black-and-white striped bull's-eyes, treacle toffees, pear drops and Everton mints. I loved the dark interiors of the shops, each with its own smells and character. Lucas's was our nearest grocery shop; a brass bell rang as the door was opened, and counters lined three sides of its large interior. On the left was the slicer, where bacon, ham and gammon were sliced; on the right, the cheese cutter where delicious, crumbly Cheddar was cut with a wire before being wrapped in greaseproof paper and popped into a brown paper bag. Mrs Lucas, at the counter in the centre, sold broken biscuits for a penny per quarter pound and was very popular with the village children.

Opposite Lucas's was the War Memorial, where the names of dead men who had fought in the First and Second World Wars were inscribed on a brass plaque and where wreaths of poppies were laid each memorial day. I found that ceremony very moving, and still do. I always place coins in the collecting boxes today in tribute to those brave, gallant young men who gave their lives for King and country, and endured inhuman suffering before falling foul of a sniper's bullet or an exploding shell. Those who survived and returned home were usually so emotionally and spiritually damaged by their experiences that they never spoke of them, and fought their demons in nightmares of unspeakable horror. They lived for decades with these grotesque burdens.

The architecture in Byfleet was eclectic to say the least. Our house was built in the 1930s, as were a number of the bungalows that filled the streets nearby. But there were also Edwardian and Victorian villas: not large, but generating a sense of history and past lives – lives lived not so very differently from our own; along with a generous supply of council houses for those unable to imagine the possibility of owning their own home, but able to afford the modest rental required by the local council.

I also discovered my passion for craftsmanship in my childhood. Most of the shop interiors were late Victorian or early Edwardian, my favourite being Garnet-Jones in West Byfleet. I remember the glass-topped, gleaming mahogany counter where you could purchase undergarments, and the glass handles on the drawers of silk petticoats, nylon stockings and lacy nightdresses in the softest of materials, nestling seductively in the finest of tissue paper. When you had selected your items, you were handed a bill at the counter by the charming lady who had served you. It was handwritten and had a little drawing of a shepherdess with a parasol in the top left-hand corner. The bill and money were put into a small cylinder attached to a wire suspended from the ceiling and whizzed down to the end of the shop to be met by a cashier –

also charming – positioned behind a partition with an oval arch in the glass front. She would extract both money and bill from the cylinder, stamp the bill as a receipt, pop it back into the container along with change if necessary, and whizz it back to the sales lady. I found this entire process fascinating, and have yet to be convinced that the checkout counters in Tesco et al are an improvement on Garnet-Jones.

So my memories of Byfleet are soft, with my love of nature, the rhythms of the countryside, the changing seasons and the gentleness of life before the tower blocks of the sixties heralded the destruction of communities that had existed for hundreds of years.

In the early sixties, when women began taking the contraceptive pill, society changed forever. With control over their fertility for the first time in history, women began to venture into the workplace, discover financial independence, and study for a career as opposed to taking a job which would terminate when they married. They had the same sexual freedom as men and were determined to enjoy their newfound liberation.

As communities began to disintegrate and rows of terraced workmen's cottages fell foul of the bulldozer, to be replaced with the anonymity of soulless tower blocks, so too did the television set usurp the fireplace. No longer did families gather together of an evening to sit around the fire. Reading, listening to the wireless and conversation were replaced by that miracle of modern technology, the television set. My father purchased one for the Queen's coronation. So great was his excitement at being able to watch moving pictures, with sound, in his own 'lounge' that he came into my bedroom, woke me from a deep sleep and insisted I come and see it. I was nine years old and, as established earlier, my bed was my kingdom and my refuge; and as I became quite hysterical when roused from the depths of sweet oblivion, my introduction to this marvel of the twentieth century was less than auspicious. I loathed it on sight which, in retrospect, was probably an extremely healthy response.

So much for Byfleet, my love of nature and the feel of the times. I suppose now is the time to set down why I didn't like the *life* I lived there.

～

My immediate family history is not without a certain complexity. For the first six months of my life, our house was occupied by my parents, Reginald and Stella Pearce, and myself. In June of 1944, in an attempt to make some much-needed extra money, my father advertised the front room and a bedroom for rent. My father was exempt from war service due to his employment at Vickers Armstrong, a factory involved with the manufacturing of aircraft, which were frequently blown up by the enemy when they left the factory and took to the air. (Although my father didn't see active service during the war years, I understand he did some sterling work in the Home Guard.)

His advertisement was answered by a young woman in her twenties, May Wilcox, whose husband George was fighting the enemy as a member of the Royal Navy. She accepted the rooms, moved in and was joined on his occasional spells of home leave by George. So the house now contained two families: the Pearces and the Wilcoxes.

Ten months later, my mother, having decided that domesticity was not for her, left my father and myself in search of more exciting pastures. After discussion with May, a decision was reached. She would write to George and, if he agreed, when the war ended they would both live with us; she as housekeeper/substitute mother, he to continue his pre-war work in some clerical capacity, also at Vickers Armstrong. George would also become my legal guardian in the event of my father's demise. So they assumed the roles of foster parents. I called May Mother, her husband Uncle, and my father, Father.

May was childless, and had no idea how to care for a baby; my father had to teach her everything. He had given me bottles himself since my birth, as my mother, apparently reluctant to lose her figure, disposed of her milk at the kitchen sink as he did so. Pity that, as I understand that breast feeding gives the odd benefits: strengthened immune system, a close bond with the mother, a sense of security which creates confidence and leads to a feeling in later life of having an authentic position in the world.

My father was the penultimate of ten children, born in West Ham in the East End of London, and his life's ambition was to escape the poverty and overcrowding of his childhood. He was a natural gentleman and extremely dapper. One of his brothers, Sidney, proved himself an excellent tailor, and throughout his life my father was impeccably turned out in the handmade suits supplied by Uncle Sidney. I never saw him look anything less than elegant: he was an extremely fastidious man, and sported a slim black moustache which, combined with a full head of jet-black hair and dark brown eyes, made him a rather attractive man. He always had difficulty accepting his height – five feet four and a half – and never, I felt, fulfilled his true potential.

He was an excellent craftsman. During the war and for some time after, it was very difficult to find paint. He had carved two elephants for me and painted them green, it being the only colour available. I still have them and I wish so much he could have pursued his talents as an artisan, and not the role of businessman to which he was totally unsuited.

I can't claim to have known my father; he rarely spoke of his childhood, and never about his emotional life. He was the product of a Victorian upbringing, and mine was the last generation to grow up under the constraints a Victorian influence imposed. Mine was definitely a 'children should be seen and not heard' childhood; decisions concerning me were never discussed with me, and my father's choice of school was based not on the education I would receive there, but on the principle that the convent would ensure that I became a lady. Although I can't claim to have known him, and our relationship was never a close one – I was too afraid of him for that – I intuited him, unaware that I was doing so, and absorbed a great deal of his pain, which added to my own from a very young age.

The loss of my mother at the age of sixteen months was the defining moment of my life. It has informed everything I have been and become. Its influence might have become less intense in later life, had I successfully bonded with May; the insecurity I experienced might not have been as chronic. After my mother's departure, I was sent to a nursery, my only memory of it being one of potty training. I was placed on a pot and told to 'do my business' which I consciously refused, being at some level aware that I suddenly had a hold over the adult whose demands I declined to fulfil. However, the legacy of this rebellion was acute constipation which persisted for quite some years.

When the war ended, George came to live permanently with us and May was no longer required to work outside the home. Just before my third birthday I was sent to stay with my father's sister, Auntie Win, who lived with her husband, Uncle Fred, in Upminster, Essex. I loved staying with Auntie Win; she had one child herself, my cousin Peter, who being ten years older occupied a different planet. Auntie Win loved having a little girl around, and spent hours twisting my long, dark brown hair around strips of rag, which would result in ringlets when she removed them the following morning. The love, kindness and attention that Auntie Win showed me during those difficult early years is something I have never forgotten.

When I returned to Byfleet, after having spent Christmas and my third birthday in Upminster, it was to discover that May and George had had their own child, a daughter called Maxine; her impending birth being the reason for my stay in Upminster. No one had told me that this was on the cards, so I arrived home to find that I had lost my substitute mother to her own child; then, I feel, my problems began in earnest.

May was a woman who, by her own admission, lacked imagination. This made her unable to realise that I was traumatised by the events of my life thus far. To lose one mother is perhaps a sustainable loss; to lose two and emerge unscathed is, I suggest, asking a little too much. The problem was also compounded by the fact that watching her relationship with her own child enabled me to see what I was missing.

The foundations upon which my life were built were flimsy to say the least, and completely unable to support me as I grew; the wound I carried from the loss of maternal love was unable to heal, and became bigger than I was and overwhelmed me from a very early age. It expressed itself in a chronic insecurity, and a lifelong battle with pain and depression.

So, by the age of three, I had lost not only my birth mother but also my substitute mother, and been farmed out to the nursery from April 1945 for what remained of the duration of the war. And with a 'mother' whose husband I called 'Uncle', and a 'sister' I called Maxine, all bearing a different surname to me, and a father who wasn't married to my 'mother', my home life was unlike that of any of my contemporaries, who appeared to have far more orthodox set-ups. I was also born left-handed which I was forced to change; much later in life I discovered this was because my birth mother was also left-handed, and my father wanted no evidence of her in me at all. Quite a tall order that, as fifty per cent of my genetic make-up was hers. Much later, it was discovered that forcing left-handed children to become right-handed, besides interfering with right-brain/left-brain function, makes them evolve into very confused adults. I have absolutely no ability with practical matters – technology defeats me, handy around the home I am not – and if you are forced to change something that feels intrinsically right, the message you carry into later life is: if it feels right, it must be wrong. You can appreciate the potential for confusion. (Although, having said that, a friend who had a similar experience is artistically gifted, has a degree in computer science, can build a house, restore classic American cars, learn a complex language in twenty minutes flat and practically anything else you care to mention.) I do know that I'm astoundingly lacking in many key areas of life.

My father was not a happy man, and his dis-ease was manifested in the form of stomach ulcers and debilitating back pain. His health was quite fragile, and operations on his ulcers only provided temporary relief, as they always grew back. He was an extremely strict parent. So terrified was he that I would resemble my mother in later life that he held on very tightly to his own idea of who he wanted me to become. In later life I grew to understand that, whatever else he wanted me to be, he didn't want me to be in any way a sexual being. And by sending me to a convent, he very nearly obtained his wish. I think he found my mother's sexuality threatening, and believed at some level that his inability to satisfy her sexually was a large factor in her decision to leave him. I understand she had a predilection for American GIs with their access to nylon stockings, chocolate and chewing gum. She found their accents, and the aura of American movies that she projected onto them, extremely glamorous and romantic; and Boston had to be more exciting than Byfleet.

My father was a man of integrity, and a product of the values of his time. Although he very rarely discussed my mother with me, he did tell me that his decision to marry her was due to her telling him that she was pregnant. He duly 'did the right thing' and, on the top deck of the bus taking them home after the marriage ceremony at West Ham Registry Office, she told him that she was not in fact pregnant after all. When I asked him why he continued with the marriage after discovering he had been duped, he said that he had made his bed, and now he must lie on it. So that was that.

My feeling is that he was powerfully attracted to her physically, a feeling that wasn't reciprocated; and what they had in common was limited. Many years later, a meeting with my half-sister, conceived three years after my mother left my father, provided me with information about my mother that allowed me to fill in a few of the many missing pieces to that particular puzzle. For the first fifteen years of her life Patricia, my half-sister, lived with our mother before she once again left hearth and home for greener pastures, never to be seen again. Our mother, it seems was an enigma. A fantasist and compulsive liar; beautiful; given to changing her name and hair colour on a weekly basis; a drama queen *par excellence*, and with eyes that apparently 'had no soul'. Patricia said that although I greatly resembled her physically, the enormous difference between us was that *my* eyes *did* 'have soul.' (Phew!) She wasn't at all surprised that one of our mother's offspring had decided on a theatrical career.

But the information I found most extraordinary was the discovery that my mother was a pure-blooded Romany gypsy! This explained so much about myself that had previously been inexplicable. My ideal home has always been a Romany caravan with an en-suite bathroom. My mother's family were not travellers, but lived in a settled community in the East End of London which still, I understand, exists today. Patricia had many memories of going to stay with our Aunt Britannia, our mother's sister, who lived in a traditional Romany caravan, decorated in rich reds, blues and gold, and with an abundance of velvet cushions and brocaded curtains. My own capacity for transforming any home I have lived in into a Romany caravan is legendary among my friends: when I was living on a houseboat in Chelsea, I was visited for the first time by a young boy with Down's Syndrome. He came down the stairs to the sitting room/galley, looked around and said, 'It looks like a gypsy lives here, where's yer crystal ball?'

My mother's talent for drama was another genetic inheritance. I only met her twice. As a child I'd had a dream that my mother would pass by a theatre, see my photograph outside, find me, and we would live together happily ever after.

The first three parts of the dream came true, but the final one eluded me. When I finally met her at the age of thirty-three it was to discover that we had no common ground, there was nothing to suggest we were connected and that her intention was to exploit me financially.

When I was eleven, I was peeing into the loo when I saw that the water had become red with blood – *my* blood – and it was coming from between my legs, and my knickers were stained and sodden; neither May nor the nuns had seen fit to give me any instruction regarding menstruation. It must have been a Monday: May was passing clothes through the wringer of her recently acquired washing machine as I flew into the kitchen in a state of terror. I explained as well as I could the source of my fear.

'Oh,' said May, 'that'll be your period; I thought the girls at school would have told you about it.'

Well they hadn't, Mommy dearest; and surely that was your responsibility? In any case, I began menstruating much earlier than most of my classmates who started around thirteen or fourteen, so it wasn't something we would have discussed as it was outside our experience. She gave me a sanitary towel, and a sanitary belt, and that was my introduction into the mysterious world of femininity.

I don't blame May for her lack of sensitivity at such a difficult time in my life, or for her lack of imagination, or her jealousy of me, but I did feel great anger towards her later in my life – as I did also for her habit, when I had misbehaved in some way, of saying, 'Just you wait until your father gets home, my girl, just you wait.' These were the days when corporal punishment for children was still considered perfectly normal. My father would tell me to go to my room, and then chase me up the stairs, hitting me on each tread. May found this hilarious, and I would hear her laughing in the 'lounge' each time my father's heavy hand made contact with my bare legs.

A few months later, I left a used sanitary towel in the bathroom; it was wrapped and ready to be disposed of in the kitchen boiler, but I had forgotten to take it with me, and it was discovered by my father shortly after I had left it. So great was his anger that he took me into the garden and hit me. I often wondered what had provoked this rage, which seemed out of proportion to my offence; according to the psychiatrist I discussed it with later in life, what my father was trying to beat out of me was the evidence of my burgeoning sexual maturity. He wanted me to remain his 'little girl'.

My relationship with my father also contained a strong element of sexuality, albeit unconscious. Ours was not a large house: two bedrooms and a box room – mine – so when members of the Pearce family arrived to stay for Christmas, my father would vacate his double bed for the duration, and sleep with me on my single-sized horsehair mattress. Two warm bodies, connected by blood, experiencing the enforced intimacy of a single bed, drew great comfort from that intimacy, each in his/her own way. I longed to have this warmth with my father forever, to have him exclusively for myself, to stay in this cocoon of togetherness for all eternity. To always feel this safe, this protected by the father in whose arms I lay. Oh! 'Daddy, daddy, daddy, love me, love me, *love me!*'

I understand that any sexual feelings my father harboured for me were not in fact an indication of paedophilia, or of an intent to turn desire into deed. The reasons for not encouraging physical union between immediate family members are not moral, but biological: it weakens the species, and any offspring resulting from the union will be fragile, probably deformed, and will not enjoy a good quality of life; so it appears eminently reasonable not to encourage it. And also, daddy is mummy's man, so it makes more sense to get one of your own. But, in my case, mummy wasn't there; only me and daddy, which tends to cast a different light on the matter. But my father was in no way equipped to deal with sexual feelings towards his own daughter, particularly when she was only seven years old. He was far too intellectually impoverished to understand, and was appalled by his feelings for me. This explains the many times he hit me: unable to accept that he had what he considered to be completely inappropriate feelings for his daughter, he transferred his disapproval of himself onto me and tried to beat it out of me.

May's feelings for me were complex. Her affair with my father started before I was ten. When I was eleven George was diagnosed with tuberculosis, probably contracted during his Navy years; he spent a year in a sanatorium as a result. It was during his absence that I became aware of the relationship between May and my father. One night I went downstairs for a glass of water, heard sounds coming from the lounge, opened the door and discovered them *in flagrante delicto*. The discovery was never mentioned, nor the time I met her coming out of my father's bedroom clad in nothing but some rather fetching underwear. The following – brief – conversation took place:

'What were you doing in daddy's bedroom?'

'I was closing his curtains for him.'

'Why couldn't he close them himself?'

'Go to bed, it's very late.'

'Yes, it's two o'clock and it's dark.'

'*Go to bed!*'

I realised then that they were more than 'just good friends'.

My father was a much better provider than George which enabled him to give me elocution, tennis and swimming lessons. May, of course, wanted the same for Maxine, but George was unable to come up with the readies. So she became jealous of me as well as pissed off with him. I was also artistically gifted which Maxine wasn't. But I think her quite remarkable lack of imagination was responsible for a lot of her behaviour and attitudes towards me. I asked her once who she loved best, Maxine or me? 'Maxine, of course,' was her reply. When I discussed this with her many years later, she denied having said it. 'I wouldn't say something like that,' she stated categorically. 'Okay,' I said, 'let's assume you didn't say it. Why have I gone through decades believing that you did? Could it have been something in your attitude perhaps?' The scene is as clear in my mind as on the day she said it, as I know she did! I have absolutely no animus towards my birth mother or my father, but I have to confess to frequently feeling less than charitable towards May.

During my mid teens I started to show evidence of my mental turmoil. I arrived home from school one day to find May in a state of extreme anger. When my father failed to appear for his tea, I asked her where he was. 'I don't know,' was her response. 'When will he be back?' I insisted. She then told me he had gone off with Vi, the barmaid who worked in the Queens Head, and she had no idea when or if he would return. May's anger, of course, stemmed from the fact that she herself had been having a covert affair with my father for many years, and knowing he was with another woman made her both angry and extremely jealous. My father remained absent for two weeks, and the night he returned, I was in bed. He came into my room and gave me a box of chocolates. I hurled them through the open window, and screamed at him, 'I don't want chocolates, I want *you*!' I then began to keen like an animal, my terror of losing my lone parent so great that I was oblivious to anything else. My anger, fear and isolation engulfed me, and spewed out of me like the demons they were.

I have great compassion for my father; he punished both of us endlessly for his perceived crime, and suffered greatly as a result. But it did leave me with enormous sexual problems. During my first marriage, on the few occasions when intercourse was attempted, the image of my father that always appeared in the top left-hand corner of my mind was definitely a passion killer. Sex was forever associated with my father; and, not having the insight I have since accrued, at the time I experienced this as a terrifying perversion: how could I possibly equate sex with my father – this was wholly unacceptable, a crime against Nature? My sexual responses were nil, I found the act itself extremely painful – I was a tad tense which could of course explain that – and the combined influences of paternal and religious guilt were to torment me for many years to come. What tangled webs we weave.

To add to the confused relationship I had with my father, George also presented me with problems. One evening when I was about fourteen, May and my father had gone to a Masonic dinner in London, and George and I were washing up the tea things in the kitchen. Suddenly he said to me, 'Do you know what a French kiss is?' I nodded my head, surprised by the question as sex was never mentioned in our household. 'Would you like to give me one?' was his next question. I shook my head vehemently, and left the room.

George used to wake me early in the morning so I could reluctantly crawl from the warmth of my bed in time to do my paper round. One morning I lay awake with my eyes still closed when I heard him enter the room. He didn't immediately wake me, but instead went to the end of the bed where the clothes I had worn the previous day lay in a tangled heap. He sorted through them, picked out my knickers and smelt them. I never let him know that I had witnessed this, and it happened again and again. One evening when I was taking a bath, Angie, my best friend, was in the bathroom with me. There was an attic room which connected May and George's room to the bathroom. Ange used to sit on the loo, and idly open and shut the door on the bathroom side. As she was doing so, she suddenly screamed and ran to the end of the bathroom. She had opened the attic door to discover George lying naked, watching me through a crack under the door, masturbating as he did so. He also used to give me letters which supposedly had been written by a young boy with whom he shared an office. They went into great detail concerning the sexual fantasies he had about me; and both Ange and I knew that they had been written by George himself.

By this time, I had a circle of male friends whom I met with Ange, usually in the Byfleet Recreation Ground (the 'Rec'). My first boyfriend was Arthur Luce, who with his cornflower blue eyes and hair the colour of deepest jet attracted my attention. Of course, I wasn't allowed to have boyfriends, so elaborate subterfuge had to be employed. I also had a friend who was the daughter of the local policeman, and so lived in the 'cop shop'. One night I told my father I was going to visit her, and yes, I would be home by eight o'clock. In fact I met Arthur: we cycled up to 'Lovers' Lane' as it was called – and very beautiful it was too – parked our bikes against an oak tree, and stole, hand in hand, into the depths of the wood that lined one side of the track and kissed. (Nothing more you understand; I was a 'good girl'!) By the time I had arrived back at the cop shop and turned my bike around, I met my father coming up the cop shop path. That was an *extremely* close shave, and I must have fancied Arthur rotten to have risked my father's ire in such a major way.

The other boyfriend I remember was Robin Elkins, whose father owned a well-stocked sweet shop at the end of the village. I decided to leave home, and left a note saying that I refused to return until/unless I was treated like an adult. I packed a small suitcase and rode, unsteadily, on my bike to the Rec. I told a friend that I had left home, and would he please go and get Rob for me, so we could run away together. The friend duly delivered the message and returned with Rob's response which was, 'Could it wait until tomorrow night, as I'm doing my English homework?' Then, to add insult to injury, Mr Elkins phoned my father who appeared in the Rec to take me home, in disgrace, in front of all my mates. (A bitter pill.)

Once every two years, on Parish Day – a big deal let me tell you – a travelling fair would descend and establish itself in a large green swathe in the Rec. I loved the fairground with its amplified music blaring out the pop songs of the day, the cloying sweetness of candyfloss and toffee apples, the delicious smells of frying onions and hamburgers, the lights on the carousel flashing pink, yellow, electric blue and green. But most of all I loved the sense of adventure that it brought with it: of lives lived in caravans whose curtained windows concealed cosiness and warmth. And the boys... I was fascinated by the boys with their thick black hair, slick with grease, sporting muscular arms from their sleeveless vests, and equally muscular legs encased in the tightest of blue jeans as the wooden platforms on which they plied their trade moved sinuously, in time to the accompanying sounds of Pat Boone, Johnnie Ray, the Platters and Gene Pitney. I always felt a sense of loss when the fair moved on, as though it had taken part of me with it. No doubt the reality of living with the fair contained far less glamour and romance than I had invested it with, but glamour and romance were what I yearned for. (My mother's daughter...)

I was the child of atheists who were strictly christening, marriage and funeral churchgoers. I was baptised in the Protestant church (quite why, I have no idea – perhaps my father decided to keep my options open) and then dispatched to a Catholic convent for my schooling. I believe my father's choice was made because the only other option afforded by the small village of Byfleet was the local primary school, which my father felt would not provide the manners and decorum that the convent assuredly would. My father's ambition for me was that I should be a 'lady' above all else, and to this end I was sent suitably suited and booted to the Marist Convent, West Byfleet at the beginning of the spring term in January 1948, a matter of a few weeks after my fourth birthday.

2
The Convent Years

The convent years. I could dispose of them in one sentence. I hated every single solitary moment of the thirteen years of what passed for my 'education', with a loathing I retain to this day.

My uniform consisted of a pleated navy-blue gymslip worn over a white Viyella blouse, a navy and yellow striped tie knotted at its neck; a navy-blue cardigan, fawn knee-length socks and robust, brown lace-up shoes. A dark navy-blue coat and the dreaded navy-blue felt hat with yellow and navy ribbon adorning the brim completed this fetching ensemble. I was taken to the school gate by my father and deposited in a state of primal terror into the hands of what appeared to be an extremely large penguin. I had never seen a nun before and a little preparation for what this entailed would have been appreciated.

Because May had Maxine to look after, it had been decided that I would remain at the convent all day, taking my dinner there and returning home at the end of the school day at four p.m. My most potent memories of the three years for which I maintained this regime are of the disgustingness of what passed for the midday meal. The smell of undercooked, waterlogged potatoes, the 'eyes' of which were never removed, the gristle that accompanied the unidentifiable meat portion, the soggy cabbage and the tapioca that represented pudding remain with me to this day. All meals had to be eaten in their entirety; failure to do so resulted in remaining at the table until the plate had been cleared to the satisfaction of the nun on dinner duty. I frequently found myself staring mutinously at my uneaten meal until forced to eat something, at which point I would immediately vomit. This routine continued until I was dismissed as a hopeless, rebellious child who required disciplining until she could behave in the manner expected of a modest convent girl. Once Maxine started school at the age of five (May refusing to surrender her until legal obligations made her attendance mandatory) I was spared these horrors and returned with Maxine to the family home to partake of the midday meal. My resentment of Maxine's preferential treatment rankled for many years.

Although non-Catholics like myself were supposed to receive religious instruction independently of the Catholic girls, in reality there was very little difference. All lessons began and ended with prayers and I quickly became familiar with the Hail Marys, Our Fathers and Glory Be's of the daily routine and joined the crocodile of girls as we made our way to the chapel on feast days and holidays of obligation. The chapel was in the convent house, where the nuns lived independently of the two school buildings where we received our education. It was cool and seemed always to be in shadow; the floors were highly polished and the scent of beeswax was comforting and somehow reassuring. The chapel was dominated by the gold cross on which hung the crucified body of Our Lord. The pews were hard and, without the protection afforded by the voluminous skirts of the nuns, our exposed knees shrieked with protest through endless decades of the rosary.

So from the age of four I was subjected to the indoctrination of Catholic dogma, and wrestle with its malign influence to this day. But I loved the incense, the ritual, the music and sheer showmanship that the Catholic Church provides with such zeal. I was easily seduced, and my desire to belong was so great that I participated willingly in the nuns' attempts to convert my heathen soul.

I moved from Kindergarten to Transition, and on to Form One at the age of seven. I was a bright child and, with good teachers, would have responded well to education. I had no talent for maths but had a love of literature and history. However, lacking teachers who could make these subjects come alive, I was left very much to my own devices and my reading lacked guidance as I devoured whatever I could lay my hands on at the local library. I had learned to read at the age of three and could read and write quite well, my father retaining letters I had written him at that age when I had been sent to stay with his sister during May's confinement. I regret that my innate intelligence wasn't nurtured and developed and feel my lack of academic achievement to this day.

Reading was and remains one of my great passions, although I use it as an escape more than a means of enlightenment and knowledge. No matter what my circumstances may be, how desperate my situation at the time, a book provides a holiday from reality. And I take many, many holidays! Although, having said that, I have learned much from books; great, good, bad and indifferent books all have something to teach me, something that resonates and increases my small store of knowledge and greatly enhances my pleasure. The only times I have been unable to escape from reality into the alternative options provided by books have been during my spells of severe depression: then, concentration was impossible and I could do nothing but submit to the darkness that engulfed me.

I became a clock-watcher at a very early age. Mondays I approached with fear and trembling, Tuesdays were marginally better and dinnertime on Wednesdays brought a sigh of relief as it meant we were half way through the school week. Thursdays were welcome, being the day before Friday, and release from school for two whole days! I'd climb onto the bus at four o'clock thinking, 'Hip hip hooray! Three whole nights and not a fuckin' nun in sight.'

I think the nuns disliked me so much because I was the child of divorced parents; divorce was almost unheard of in the late 1940s and they were concerned that the Catholic girls would be tainted by the aura of mortal sin that surrounded me. I was also in a state of original sin due to not having been baptised in the one true church and, until or unless I was, I was destined for the fiery pit, as were my parents due to their divorce. This prognosis effectively wiped out my branch of the Pearce family.

At the age of seven I was sent to Miss Nurse – a lay teacher at the convent – for elocution lessons; and this extraordinarily talented woman was to prove a huge influence in my life. Her married name was Ivy Mears, but her husband always called her Nan (she called him Humpy) and I was encouraged to call her Nanny. Nanny had trained to be an actress at the Central School of Speech and Drama under the auspices of Miss Elsie Fogerty, a fact of which she was justifiably proud. Great emphasis was placed on voice production, and that was my weak area, having a tendency to speak in the back of my throat and swallow my vowels. Nanny had had ambitions to be an actress herself and was extremely talented, but her eyesight was weak and she had to wear thick spectacles in order to see with anything approaching clarity, it being long before the days of contact lenses. This proved too great a handicap for the stage, and so she abandoned her dream of a life in the theatre and became instead a great teacher.

I loved Nanny dearly and she loved me in return. She recognised my talent for drama, and did everything in her power to nurture it. She went so far as to ask my father if she could adopt me; he refused, but I wish he hadn't. I would have benefited so much under her influence, in an environment so rich in literature, culture and the arts. Nanny took me to Stratford-upon-Avon to the Shakespeare Memorial Theatre to see Peggy Ashcroft playing Rosalind in *As You Like It*, my first experience of 'real' theatre; my previous outings were to pantomimes at Christmas. When my dream of a career as a dancer turned to ashes, it was very easy to switch my attention from dance to drama and this ambition Nanny greatly encouraged.

After the sanitary towel incident my father also terminated my ballet, tennis and elocution lessons. Miss Nurse refused to accept that my lessons were to be ended, and asked my father to come to the convent in order to discuss the situation. What passed between them was never disclosed, but my elocution lessons continued unabated. Nanny was the one person in my corner, my one support during my years at the convent, indeed throughout my childhood; she died from angina when I was twenty-three and living in Los Angeles, and I miss her to this day.

My talent for drama was to bring me many medals and trophies with which to adorn the convent mantelpiece. The reaction of the nuns to my dramatic successes was ambivalent: they enjoyed the kudos of my achievements, but were dubious as to the choice of roles Nanny selected for me. I once performed a duologue from the recently premiered John Osborne play *Look Back in Anger*, the play which revolutionised and transformed the theatre in London, and outraged much of middle England in the process. It was the scene when Alison returns to the flat after she has lost her baby, and has a confrontation with Helena – her best friend, and now her husband's lover – which was viewed with horror by both the nuns and May. 'Why don't you do Shakespeare, something you know you can do,' was May's reaction, 'and not this immoral piece of rubbish you're rehearsing at the moment.' Never having seen or read the play, her opinions were those of the popular press, not the result of independent thought.

However, Nanny, Denise Thorn (Helena) and I ploughed on regardless, and on the day we performed it at the Woking Drama Festival I had one of those magic moments which have only occurred twice in my life. During the actual performance I transcended myself – touched something in me that connected with the source of my talent – as though not I but something greater were speaking through me. Much to the chagrin of the nuns, Den and I won that day; and the adjudicator wrote of my performance, 'If ever one dare forecast these things, this is one of the most promising young actresses it is possible to see.' The other time I experienced this connection with the source of my talent was with the same play, performing Alison's final speech during a class when I was a student at RADA. It was directly as a result of Nanny's influence that I was allowed to audition for the Royal Academy of Dramatic Art.

The one thing about the convent which gave me a great deal of pleasure was the school buildings themselves. The school was Edwardian and purpose-built to be a school. The classrooms, each containing twenty pupils, were large, airy spaces, each containing a fireplace (unfortunately never used); the door handles and door plates were made of brass, the banisters of carved wood, the ceilings adorned with intricate mouldings, and the craftsmanship and care generated a warmth and harmony, supplied a sense of security. I understand that it was pulled down some years ago and replaced with the kind of cold, impersonal, brick and concrete structures so prevalent today. Such a travesty.

My relationship with the nuns diminished greatly as I advanced in years, my father being interviewed by Reverend Mother on several occasions due to my propensity for telling 'immoral stories' and refusing to wear the dreaded felt hat – panama in summer – in the street. I also had the audacity to be physically mature by the age of eleven, and all evidence of sexuality had to be stamped on at any price. Girls were, after all, the daughters of Eve and bore all the responsibility for the sexual behaviour of men, who were very prone to the temptations of the flesh which had to be kept in check no matter what the cost. We were forbidden to be alone with the parish priests, had to avert our eyes when the gardener was mowing the lawns and be chaste at all times. But when adolescence arrived and the priests were confronted with billowing breasts, school frocks stained with overflowing menstrual blood and the air scented with burgeoning sexuality, the nuns' agitation went into overdrive. Sex was permitted only within the context of marriage and for the sole purpose of procreating the human race. St Maria Goretti was our heroine, a young girl of fourteen who was murdered because she refused to submit to the base attentions of an overly enthusiastic male. Many of the girls in my year left the convent with huge sexual hang-ups; I myself was totally frigid for more years than I care to remember, a condition which resulted in the demise of both my marriages, and a small fortune in psychiatrists' fees. But I remained chaste whenever I was chased.

I particularly loathed Sister Columbiere – Claude to us girls – who 'taught' English and History, and Sister Concessa – Connie – who 'taught' French, and I believe my feelings were entirely mutual. Connie had a red face, small brown eyes, a large nose and a propensity for hitting the backs of legs with a ruler should homework be neglected. Mine frequently felt the sting of the ruler, with large bumps and red marks appearing as a result. Of course my transgressions had little to do with vocabulary and much to do with my overt sexuality, but I only recognised this with hindsight.

Claude was a tall, angular being, pale of complexion and possessed of a large nose upon which perched a pair of black-framed spectacles and which displayed a dewdrop dangling precariously from its tip during the long winter months. As far as Claude was concerned I was the spawn of Satan and to be dealt with accordingly; I was solely responsible for any transgressions which occurred in class and on one particular occasion when she had left the room for some reason and returned to find it in uproar, her first words were, 'Jacqueline Pearce, I might have known it.' I happened to be standing behind her at the time having left the classroom to go to the cloakroom in her absence and about to re-enter it as she returned. My delight when she realised her error remains with me to this day. Her lack of talent as a teacher was quite extraordinary; she managed to make Jane Austen appear pedestrian, Dickens boring and Shakespeare incomprehensible. A remarkable achievement.

The other lay teacher who made a great impression on me was Mrs Watson who was employed to teach PE. We were hauled out in all weathers to play hockey and netball in the bleak winter months. I was remarkably lacking in talent for any kind of sport, and changed into the dreaded shorts required to perform them with all the enthusiasm of a doomed prisoner *en route* to his date with destiny. I hated the cold – and English winters in the 1950s were *seriously* cold. As I shivered on the netball court, Mrs Watson, attired in her warm track suit, thick cosy scarf and woolly hat, would shout encouragement from the sidelines whilst liberally and frequently applying copious quantities of hand cream. She would also pick two girls to be leaders of the teams and would then instruct them to pick the rest of their team from the remaining girls. Not surprisingly, given my lack of talent and enthusiasm for all things sporting, I would be left until last which did nothing for my confidence and confirmed my lack of popularity with the rest of the class. It also left me with a lifelong loathing of being exposed to inclement weather and anything resembling physical activity. Not for me a brisk, invigorating walk in the park; I want a good book, a roaring fire and blessed warmth. I loved the photographer David Bailey's definition of exercise as, 'playing chess with the window open'. Nice one Bailey.

It's possible that a very few of the nuns were there because they had a genuine religious vocation, but for the most part I believe they were there because they were unable to find a chap to settle down with and so joining a convent was probably the only gig open to them. Their repressed sexuality was damaging to themselves, and certainly to their pupils. There was a seething undercurrent of rage in Sister Concessa, communicated to us girls via her ruler attacks, excessive amounts of homework and constant erosion of our fragile self-esteem. Despite the lack of positive role models, in my mid teens I decided I wanted not only to convert to Catholicism but also to become a nun – anything for acceptance. My father refused to allow me to convert for which I remain eternally grateful, and I think my desire to become a bride of Christ had a lot to do with seeing Audrey Hepburn in *The Nun's Story* and very little to do with a religious vocation. I wanted to go to the Congo, play with monkeys, waft around in a white habit and meet a version of Peter Finch. I realised later that, much as I loved the frock, the hours wouldn't suit.

But I continued to attend mass most mornings before school, and benediction after school on Wednesdays. I was not allowed to join 'The Legion of Mary' because I wasn't a Catholic, and of course was unable to receive communion for the same reason. I absorbed all the – considerable – guilt of Catholicism, but was denied the catharsis of confession. I would watch the girls leave the confessional box, say their three Hail Marys or whatever penance that father deemed appropriate and emerge cleansed of the sins which sat so heavily on my own – doomed – soul. Until I had been baptised in the Catholic church I would remain in a state of mortal sin, and the horrors of hell to which I was inevitably destined haunted my dreams for many years. Not a good prognosis really... To this day I have dreams, or should I say nightmares, about the convent. I wake up with my heart beating fit to burst, clammy with sweat and terrified. My relief when I realise it was in fact a dream and not reality is overwhelmingly sweet and I punch the air with delight and laugh out loud.

I made no close friends at the convent, but this lack was filled by my best friend Angie, who attended the secondary modern school. I smoked my first cigarette with Ange, bought my first eye shadow with her and knew the joy of shared confidences and real intimacy for the first time. She remains in my life to this day and our shared memories are sweet indeed.

3
Angie

I met Angie when I was thirteen and she fourteen. I don't remember how or where we met, but Ange has vague memories of our being introduced by a mutual friend outside Mr Stubbings's shop where we could purchase Weights or Woodbines singly or in packs of five depending on how flush we were.

What I remember very clearly is how we came to be best friends. We were walking past the local hairdresser's at the time when I said, 'Ange, will you be my best friend?'

'Are you dirty?' was her response.

'What do you mean?' I said.

'Do you let boys put their hands inside your jumper?'

'*No!*' was my horrified reaction.

'All right then,' she said, 'I'll be your best friend.' And so the deal was sealed.

I lived in Queens Avenue, and Ange lived close by in Walnut Tree Lane with her Aunt Glad, Uncle Fred and maternal grandmother, Gran. Angie's life had been blighted by the death of her mother when she was very young; her memories of her father were so distressing that to my knowledge she has never discussed them with anyone, and for her own protection was sent to live with Gran and her aunt and uncle. Aunt Glad was an imposing woman in her late fifties when I first made her acquaintance, with a rigid helmet of tightly permed grey hair, stout and with a cigarette permanently on the go. Uncle Fred had a hook for one hand – the right, I think it was. Quite how he lost half his arm and all of his hand I never discovered, but the hook was very impressive and I was convinced he had been a pirate on the high seas and had lost it during a bitter and bloody battle with customs and excise men as he attempted to smuggle illicit goods into caves in Cornwall. The real reason was undoubtedly more mundane but my fantasy was never shattered by the reality of knowing the actual circumstances. Gran was magic, and the one source of affection for Ange in an otherwise bleak childhood. Gran was tiny with a slightly hunched back which made her appear even smaller; she wore National Health glasses with pink plastic frames, behind which her eyes always twinkled; her white hair was soft as was her skin and she always wore a pink shawl around her shoulders. Both Ange and I adored her and her affection for her granddaughter was almost tangible.

5 Walnut Tree Lane was one of a small row of late-Victorian artisan's cottages; two up and two down, with a lean-to scullery attached to its side. The butler's sink had a cold tap and that was it. The 'lavvie' was outside and always scrupulously clean although you would freeze your tits off when using it in the bitter winter months. The scullery contained a small mirror on the wall nearest the door and this was where I'd find Ange putting on her make-up when I went round every Sunday afternoon to collect her for our visit to the pictures in Woking: a huge excitement in our young lives. When I met Ange she had her – I think it was – right foot in plaster, having just had an operation on her toes. Although she was only fourteen she never returned to school and as soon as she hit fifteen went up to London each day to work as a shorthand typist. Ange therefore had money to spend on clothes whereas my financial resources were limited to the ten bob I made doing a paper round on Sunday mornings.

Ange was extremely pretty, a natural blonde with large blue eyes and a ready smile and possessed of enormous charm. Great legs, wonderful figure and always very much her own woman. I'd push open the door and there she'd be smelling of toothpaste, tobacco and face powder and I'd watch her as she finished putting on her 'face'. I was forbidden to wear make-up so I'd wait until we got to the waiting room at Byfleet and New Haw Station, when on would go the eyeshadow and eyeliner and the black tights – part of my ballet kit (it being long before the days of sheer tights, and I was forbidden to wear stockings) which I was also not allowed to wear outside of class – and arm in arm we'd set off for the Ritz, the Odeon or the Gaumont depending on what was showing where.

My most vivid memory of Ange was when she wore her Italian suit: dark grey with a black stripe, tight skirt and short boxy jacket. White shoes and handbag completed the ensemble and she looked wicked! I took up the rear wearing an assortment of seriously unsuitable clothes for the occasion but felt compensated by the black tights, white lips and heavily shadowed eye make-up – my bohemian tendencies evident at an early age. We were a good contrast, me and Ange: Ange blonde and blue eyed and myself, dark with hazel eyes. If we were lucky and had a date – strictly forbidden where I was concerned – the boys in question would take us into the back row of the three-and-nines, a serious amount of money in those days, and we'd neck throughout the main feature, the second feature and the Pathé newsreel, and go to the 'ladies' during 'coming attractions'. But, no hands were allowed to make their way into forbidden places; we were good girls and determined to remain so.

On Thursday nights we went to West Byfleet to the Catholic Youth Club which was presided over by one of the two parish priests. Soft drinks only, although the air was blue with cigarette smoke. The boys would stand on one side of the room and the girls on the other. Ange and I would jive together until a couple of the boys overcame their self-consciousness – there being safety in numbers – and asked us to dance. It was outside the Youth Club that I smoked my first cigarette. I hated it and was violently sick, but persevered – ah! what lengths I would go to, to achieve the acceptance of my peers – and have been puffing away ever since, some fifty-three years, and with emphysema to prove it! We had to catch the ten o'clock bus home and stood at the bus stop in freezing weather, wearing totally unsuitable clothes, and thought little of the horrendous discomfort we endured as a result.

But the real highlight of our social life was the Addlestone Hop! It was held in a huge hall and had a live band playing all the latest hits: Bill Haley and the Comets, Gene Pitney, Roy Orbison and of course, Elvis! The boys in the band would be dressed in the fashion of the day and as they stood on the stage in their drainpipe trousers, long draped jackets, white shirts with a black shoelace tie knotted with careless ease at their necks and thick-soled suede shoes (known as 'brothel creepers') with blue, green, yellow and pink lights creating an aura of magic, sophistication, and unbelievable glamour, there wasn't a girl in the room who didn't long to catch the eye of the lead singer, drummer, lead guitarist or whichever of them had unleashed our dreams and yearnings and made us starry-eyed and longing for the love of our very own Prince Charming. Both Ange and I loved to dance and were mean jivers, but the last number of the evening was always a slow one and *had* to be danced with a boy, who would then escort us to the bus stop and – hopefully – ask us for a date for the pictures in Woking the following Sunday. Such excitement!

It was all very innocent, both Ange and I remaining virgins until we met the boys we would eventually marry; but oh! how my young, romantic, yearning self longed for life to be always like the 'last dance'. Safe and warm, wrapped in the arms of a boy tender with love, a song of love playing softly, the lights warm and low, moving as one in our cocoon of intimacy, achieving a union that was generated by our mutual longing for the 'other'; that unseen and deeply hidden presence sensed within the other, that whispered through our hearts and souls promising the bliss of wholeness, the healing of the divided self. Well, that's how it seemed to me; the boy was probably focused on whether he could get my knickers off before we reached the bus stop.

On weeknights we would go to the recreation ground in Byfleet where all the local youths would congregate and sit inside the wooden shed that provided shelter from the frequently inclement weather. Its walls were adorned with carvings: hearts with an arrow and initials of sweethearts, or the less romantic, 'Jane Smith is a slag. True.' I always had to be home at a certain time, and if I were even a minute late would be shamed by the appearance of my father in his green van, bristling with anger as he hauled me unceremoniously away from my friends. But, time permitting, Ange and I would walk home, stopping off at the local chippie where I would get a portion of chips wrapped in newspaper and Ange a portion of cockles or whelks, she being a great fan of shellfish which I couldn't abide; I would watch with wonder her evident delight as she consumed these – to my mind – disgusting molluscs. Ange disliked anything sweet, and seafood was her passion. I on the other hand couldn't pass a sweet shop without drooling.

5 Walnut Tree Lane had very steep stairs leading up to the two identical bedrooms, and I'm extremely relieved that I only had to climb them in the days when I drank nothing stronger than pineapple juice. How Victorian and Edwardian women in long skirts and corsets, with babies clasped to their lactating breasts, and probably under the influence of gin, managed them I can't imagine. Aunt Glad and Uncle Fred occupied the one on the right and Ange and Gran the identical one on the left. After Gran died, I used to stay with Ange in the large double bed where we whispered secrets to each other under the protective cover of night; those conversations were my first experience of real, as opposed to imagined intimacy, and greatly treasured as such. I loved that room: the thirties wardrobe; the bed, heavy with the weight of blankets and

covered in a candlewick bedspread; the glass lampshade; and the feeling of security I always experienced when I was with Ange. Without her support and friendship my adolescence would have been unbearable, and she remains to this day a greatly cherished friend, and one of the most important influences of my life. We only ever had 'words' on one occasion, when I was Ange's bridesmaid the day she married Geoff; she thought I exposed too much bosom and was rather miffed as a result.

I loved going to Woking more than anywhere else. We would wait excitedly for the train as it steamed into Byfleet and New Haw station, belching smoke from its chimney, its appetite ferocious for the black coal that fed it and which was constantly shovelled in on top of the white-hot coals it had already devoured. The next station was West Byfleet and, like the one we had just left, composed of only two tracks; but Woking had four tracks, a loudspeaker system, café and a confectionery kiosk. It felt huge to my teenager's eyes and full of romance: people going on exciting journeys; lovers parting or being reunited; boys being sent off to prep school, lower lips trembling, and looking so vulnerable in their short trousers, blazers and caps.

The carriages all had a corridor, and each compartment opened onto that corridor and had room for three people comfortably seated using the armrests, or four without using the armrests – which provided a less comfortable ride – on each side. There was a choice of 'Smoking', 'Non-Smoking' and 'Ladies Only' compartments. Ange and I always opted for 'Smoking' unless we didn't like the look of the other occupants in which case we'd go into 'Ladies Only'. The seats were covered in what looked like a heavy-duty velvet; the panels behind our heads were of wood, as was the frame surrounding the mirror. The luggage racks were a metal which looked like brass, the framework being covered with a strong string net to support passengers' cases and bags. The window was opened with a wide leather strap that ran its length and pulled up to open and down to close. I doubt it had changed much from the Edwardian era and was redolent of past times and finer things. At the time I was very unaware of how much craftsmanship satisfied me, the natural materials with which those artisans worked, the care and respect that went into their craft; understanding only dawned many years later as I witnessed with horror and sadness the destruction of so much labour, respect and love, to be replaced with plastic and harsh metals, devoid of all humanity.

Obviously relationships between girlfriends change when husbands and children arrive on the scene. I never had children but Ange and Geoff had two and also remained living relatively locally. My husband Drewe and I lived in London but we continued to meet as a foursome until my marriage to Drewe ended and I went to America for three years. And then my peripatetic lifestyle caused me to lose touch with Ange on several occasions for quite long periods. But I always found her again and have no intention of losing touch with her any more in the future.

I last saw her earlier this year on one of my infrequent trips to England: the first time we had seen each other for fifteen years. I met her at the station and knew her immediately. I waved enthusiastically; Ange looked first at me and then over her shoulder to see who I was waving to. Seeing no one behind her, she looked at me again, still with no hint of recognition on her face. 'Ange, it's me, Jack,' I shouted. Slowly it dawned on her that it was in fact me; she came over and we fell into each other's arms.

'But you look so different,' she said. 'I didn't recognise you. You're so little.' Having always been a big girl in my younger days, I am now very slim and have also lost an inch in height with the advancing years. She kept saying, 'You're such a little lady now,' tactfully omitting the 'old'. It was several hours later after much close scrutiny that she was able to say, 'I can see it's you now, but you look so different.' I'm convinced that if I had shown up with long black hair worn with a fringe she would have known me instantly; but, as my hair was short and auburn, it foxed her completely. Angie's hair was still in the same style and colour it had always been, so she looked pretty much as she always had.

But despite the physical alterations that time had wrought, very little else had changed. We talked and laughed as we always had, the intimacy of our initial friendship having survived unscathed with the passing of many years. Ange is now back in my life to stay, and I can only hope that she is as thrilled by that as I am!

꽃

My first ambition was to become a ballet dancer. Being a clumsy child, my father had sent me for ballet lessons, hoping they would correct this defect and I would emerge as the dainty, graceful little girl he had in mind. I loved the world of ballet, and continued to take lessons until I was thirteen. I had failed my eleven plus, but sat for something similar when I was thirteen; managing to scrape through on that occasion, I then auditioned for Camberley Ballet School. But although I had great musicality and was very expressive, my body was the wrong shape, I had very little sense of balance, and weak ankles; so it was with great regret that the Camberley Ballet School denied my application to become a student there.

But ballet – classical ballet – remains my great love; I find it so satisfying on so many levels. The stories themselves: *Swan Lake*, *Giselle*, *Sleeping Beauty*, all with their roots in mythology and magic; the haunting beauty of the music; the opulence of the costumes; the hugeness of the stage itself, transformed into a fairytale world of castles, cottages and shadowy lakes on which shines a silver crescent moon; the grandness of the theatres themselves with their seemingly endless rows of seats upholstered in red velvet, the vast curtains also in red velvet and trimmed with gold brocade; and the chandeliers dominating all, as they hover in space casting a magical, soft rainbow light over the hushed and expectant auditorium. There is a degree of theatricality in both ballet and opera that doesn't quite translate onto the stages occupied by actors, and it is that grandness and theatricality that attracts me like a moth to a flame. For a start the theatres are too vast for the vocal capabilities of most actors; they lack the intimacy required for many plays, and rarely require a full orchestra; and apart from the fact that all three disciplines take place on a stage, the world of actors is, I feel, far less 'big' than the worlds of classical ballet and grand opera.

Nanny's suggestion that I turn my focus from ballet to drama as a career option was eagerly accepted. They both took place on a stage and on a stage was where I wanted to be. I can't speak for other actors but I know my desire to work within the world of fantasy was fuelled by my desire to escape from myself: being myself was too painful, and inhabiting a world of make-believe, becoming someone else, was akin to taking a holiday away from the burden of being myself. And I felt a great sense of belonging when I was with fellow actors; they were my tribe, people with whom I shared a common bond, they accepted me as one of their own. During my frequent 'resting' periods what I missed most was the company of other actors. I love actors, and like the late, great Dame Edith Evans, I mean good actors. I saw her being interviewed on television by Bryan Forbes near the end of her life; he asked her if she liked actors. 'Oh yes!' she said. 'I love actors; *good* actors.'

I took five subjects when I sat for my GCE: English Language, English Literature, History, French and Religious Knowledge. I failed all of them with the exception of Religious Knowledge and had to resit them the following year. This resulted in my passing the remaining subjects with the exception of French. So I finally left the convent with four GCEs to my name, a lifelong resistance to organised religion in general and the Catholic religion in particular, a crippled sexuality and a seething resentment of all that I had endured at the hands of the 'brides of Christ'. The one thing I am grateful to the nuns for is that they taught me manners: I believe that any civilised society is successful because it has, as its foundation, good manners. Good manners generate a concern for one's fellow man, courtesy and respect. Once that disappears, it is soon replaced by anarchy, as is becoming increasingly evident in the society we inhabit today.

My father wanted me to do something sensible, like hairdressing, or secretarial work; and, knowing the acting profession to be notoriously insecure, he insisted I take a secretarial course – which would allow me something to fall back on – before I began my training at RADA. I learnt nothing, because I wasn't remotely interested in shorthand or typing, and spent most of my time there buying bottles of gin for the principal, who sat in a dishevelled heap in her tiny office at the top of the stairs. So when I left college six months later, it was with absolutely nothing to fall back on – a situation that has remained constant throughout my career. I don't think I have ever been referred to as sensible.

I remember my final day at the dreaded Marist Convent very clearly. I walked out of the convent gates for the last time, threw the hated hat into the nearest rubbish skip, and went to The Copper Kettle to celebrate with a cup of steaming hot coffee and a fag. Yippee! I was free!

4
RADA

My first day at the Royal Academy of Dramatic Art was at the start of the autumn term in September 1961. I travelled up from Byfleet full of excited anticipation, still unable to fully believe that I was about to start my training at the most famous drama academy in the world. But I was; it was true and I knew my life would never be the same again.

I took the train to Waterloo, the tube to Goodge Street, walked along Gower Street and finally came to the imposing doors of the Academy. They were closed as I was extremely early, but so great was my fear of being late that I felt nothing but relief that I had arrived with a full hour to spare. I had been loitering nonchalantly on the pavement for half an hour when I was joined by another early bird. He looked a lot older than me – I was seventeen – and, after introducing himself as Anthony Hopkins, he told me that due to having to do his National Service he had been unable to attend before now and hoped that being twenty-five wouldn't prove to be a disadvantage. I liked him immediately: his intensity, his Welsh accent and enormous energy made him extremely accessible and attractive.

We were joined by other 'first termers' and when the doors finally opened we entered into our joint adventure in a spirit of camaraderie and bonhomie. After seeing the registrar we checked the notice board to discover whether we were in Group A or B. I was in the same group as Tony and felt relieved to be placed with someone with whom I'd established a connection. The rest of the day passed in a blur of activity, meeting tutors and discovering the various rooms allocated to each of the disciplines we were required to master during the two years of our training. I returned to Byfleet at the end of the day exhausted but happy, and exhilarated at the prospect of travelling back to London on the morrow.

Slowly we all settled in, got to know the other members of our group, established friendships and in my case grew alarmingly 'bonny' in the students' canteen. It served the most delicious nursery food: sausages, baked beans, chips and a syrup sponge pudding with thick custard that I found irresistible. My desired weight and my greed fought a long and fruitless battle with my greed being the unquestioned winner. My weight remained a problem for many years; I seemed to be on a constant diet and longed to have the type of metabolism that could consume countless Mars bars without having the hips to prove it. Alas, 'twas not to be, and my 'bonniness' was frequently commented on by various staff members. I was going to be a leading lady, not a character actress, and due care and attention must be paid to my appearance.

I was once given a good talking-to on this subject by one of the tutors: her name was Valerie Hanson and she had been a very talented actress, but a car accident which had left her with permanent facial scarring ended her career and she now taught instead. She was reputed to be very hard on young, attractive female students, and this was certainly in evidence during our chat. She forbade me to eat anything containing sugar for the foreseeable future and said she would be 'keeping an eye on me' to make sure the desired weight loss occurred. My mortification on meeting her in the street a few days later just as I was taking a bite from a forbidden Mars bar remains with me to this day. She heaped scorn and sarcasm upon my person, deplored my obvious lack of moral fibre and the weakness of my character and predicted the demise of my career before it had even started. I disliked her intensely from that moment on and the feeling I can assure you was entirely mutual.

After classes finished for the day we would all repair to the Marlborough pub just around the corner in Torrington Place. The bar would be heaving with students discussing the events of the day and consuming half-pints of bitter. I myself didn't drink alcohol and would remain teetotal until I was thirty-five. I would sip my pineapple juice and study the activity taking place around me; I could never stay for long as I had to leave to catch the train back to Byfleet. This inability to fully partake in the social life of my peers was causing me great frustration as well as making me very tired. My father refused to countenance the idea of my living in London, and so at the start of my second term I decided to take matters into my own hands and made an appointment to see John Fernald, the then principal of the Academy. I explained my situation; he was extremely understanding and said he would write to my father and make him aware of the detrimental effect all the travelling was having on my studies and my – essential, in his opinion – social life. It worked! And before the week was out I had agreed to share a room in Chelsea with a fellow student, an American girl named Ann Stockdale.

The house was situated in a small side street called Paradise Walk and paradise it was. To be free from the restrictions of family life, to go with the gang for a curry at the local Indian, see the latest movie, visit the theatre and talk with Annie long into the night were heady pleasures indeed. But I was ill-prepared for the realities of independent life, having been shielded from its demands by both the convent and my father. The transition was too sudden and quite brutal and the inroads it made on my already fragile sense of self were to be made apparent when I entered my fifth term. But prior to that I was able to manage, unaware of the disintegration that was eroding my psyche and my spirit. The contrast between my previous life and my present one was so great that I was unable to bridge it, unable to connect the two in any way, and the separation between past and present grew ominously wider day by day. I had a reputation for being neurotic, and I thought it the most glamorous of descriptions – quite why I'm not sure, but it sounded seriously adult and intriguing and I was thrilled to discover that I had been singled out for attention, however dubious the reputation that resulted from that attention.

I worked with Tony a great deal; we were frequently cast opposite each other and worked well together. Besides being a gifted actor, Tony was a talented musician who played the piano and also composed. He composed the music for a mime piece I had to perform and the sensitivity and lyricism of the music gave a depth to my performance that was a direct response to the beauty of his composition.

After a while Annie decided she wanted to move elsewhere and so I moved in with a friend – Sarah Montgomery – who was renting a flat on Marylebone High Street. Another American, Sarah bore an uncanny resemblance to the French actress Jeanne Moreau. There was only one bedroom so I slept on the couch in the living room. Sarah was seeing a psychiatrist five days a week and was prescribed a medication known in those days as 'purple hearts'. She swore by them and when she invited me to try some I had no hesitation in swallowing the several she offered, not understanding that they were intended to be taken individually and not together. I only made the discovery when my heart rate speeded up alarmingly, resulting in a collection of broken blood vessels on the left side of my face – a blemish which remains to this day. I was extremely unworldly and remarkably lacking in common sense. One day during very cold weather I was finding comfort in a hot bath when the door opened and Sarah appeared. Her face turned ashen as she came to the end of the bath and very carefully removed the electric fire I had placed there in order to warm the room.

'What did you think would happen if it fell in?' she asked, her voice pitched noticeably higher than usual.

'I thought it would go out,' I replied, at a loss to understand why she was in such state.

'Yes, it would have gone out, and you with it,' was her response. She then explained to me why water and electricity were a pretty dodgy combo, and was unable to comprehend why this basic knowledge had obviously passed me by. It's quite possible that it had been explained to me at some point during my schooling, but I had obviously failed to absorb the information or simply didn't realise the importance of it; which makes me remarkably thick and, coupled with a lack of common sense, potentially dangerous to myself and the world at large. It's a problem that remains to this day although it has diminished somewhat. Things which are blatantly obvious to other people – for example, not putting an electric fire on the end of the bath – remain a mystery to me, and I'm frequently asked how I have managed to get through life thus far with what is viewed by others as a serious lack in my survival kit. I have often asked myself the same question and can only conclude that I have been gifted with an extremely vigilant guardian angel who has ensured my survival despite all the odds against it.

The emphasis at RADA in those days was very much on voice, an area where I was particularly weak, my voice being inflexible and stubbornly remaining in the back of my throat despite my best efforts to bring it forward. The tension that was growing daily within me was manifested in the tightness and rigidity of my speech. I was unable to express the emotions I was feeling with clarity; what I felt and what I conveyed bore only slight resemblance to my intention, and my frustration grew as my voice continued to elude my attempts to loosen and free it. Great emphasis was placed on the ability to speak the 'standard English' considered necessary for interpreting Shakespeare and indeed any classic play, modern or period, be it English, Russian or French. Regional accents among the students were eradicated despite the fact that Albert Finney, Alan Bates and Tom Courtenay had all achieved considerable fame in films that were based in the north of England and were to make dialects extremely fashionable in the very near future.

I enjoyed the acting classes where we would perform scenes from plays, and the classes in technique given by Robin Ray, a teacher who helped me greatly and gave me a confidence in myself that voice production certainly didn't! We were expected to go into the theatre when we finally left the Academy; in those days repertory companies flourished and provided an invaluable training for young actors new to the game. Television was slightly frowned upon and scant time was given to learning television or film technique. Radio was acceptable so we were taught microphone technique which would stand us in good stead were we fortunate enough to be invited to join the BBC Radio rep company. Steady money and no lines to learn!

As I continued my progression through the Academy I became aware that the mood swings I was experiencing were taking a great toll on me and fostering the reputation I had for being 'barking'. I consulted a doctor, who prescribed lithium and Valium, and hoped this would do the trick.

During my fourth term I had become friends with a student called Alexandra Malcolm. Alex was unquestionably the most beautiful girl I had ever seen: she had shoulder-length dark hair with 'flick ups', an olive skin, brown eyes, a classically straight nose and a generous mouth. She wore panstick make-up and brown eye shadow which remained perfectly in place all day – unlike my own which seemed to wander all over my face with a will of its own – with pale lips completing a picture of mysterious and captivating allure. She dressed in A-line skirts, sleeveless polo-necked tops and patent-leather shoes, all in black. I ached to look like Alex who seemed to enchant all who met her with her effortless grace and exotic beauty. I often visited her home, which was a rather grand house in Wilton Street, complete with Nanny who had looked after Alex all her life. Alex had the unquestioning self-confidence provided by her privileged background: the kind that can never be acquired by those who have not experienced the benefits of a good private education and access to a way of life that included literature, art, music and intellectual stimulation.

At the beginning of our fifth term Alex and I were called into John Fernald's office, together with another student – Lynn Ashcroft. Apparently the Belgrade Theatre in Coventry were planning a pantomime for their Christmas show and needed three students to play fairies. We three had been selected, and later in the term we headed for Coventry and our first professional engagement. We rented a flat near to the theatre; it was fortunately situated over a grocer's shop which was handy as our landlords told us to help ourselves from the deep freeze when we returned after a performance and settle up with them the next day. We were able to eat, but despite our combined – meagre – salaries unable to afford coal. This was the winter of 1962 and one of the coldest on record. We were permanently blue with cold and the only one of us to have any respite from its icy embrace was Alex. I wasn't the only class member to be seduced by her beauty; another student by the name of Simon Ward fell in love with her and she with him, so when he came to visit her in Coventry she had the huge consolation of a warm body to share her bed with as well as her heart. They married soon after leaving RADA, had three beautiful daughters – one of them the actress Sophie Ward – and have remained together to this day. Alex gave up the business and retrained as a psychotherapist and became very successful in her new career.

I was not a well girl; I was having hallucinations and generally hovering on the edge of blind panic. One night during the interval I was hallucinating – huge cockroaches and spiders were appearing in the mirror in front of me. Both these were particular phobias and in an attempt to make them disappear I swallowed a handful of pills. My intention was not to kill myself, simply to eradicate the visions. I returned to the stage for the final act of the show and woke up some hours later as my stomach was being pumped in the Coventry and Warwickshire Mental Hospital. This proved to be a particularly unpleasant experience, one I suggest avoiding if at all possible. I remained in the hospital for a further six weeks and felt only relief that I was in a protected environment and would be given treatment that would make me able to cope in the outside world, finish my training and emerge as a grounded and balanced human being. Little did I realise what lay ahead of me in the years to come, and what a long path I had to tread before I became remotely grounded or balanced.

The pantomime was directed by a young man; it was his first job and his name was Trevor Nunn. Now, I can quite understand his being somewhat piqued that the absence of one of his fairies should mar the creative genius of his production, and doubtless this pique was responsible for his failure to visit me, send flowers or even a get-well card; as far as Trev was concerned, I had not only ceased to exist but was in the best place possible for someone as emotionally disturbed as I had shown myself to be. I can also understand why he has never employed me since, and not being one to harbour grudges I completely forgive the seeming gross insensitivity of a young, fiercely ambitious genius. Love and peace Trev, love and peace. All I will say is that if he offered me employment in the future, he'd have to beg me, on his knees. And do me a favour while he was down there. Only joking Trev, honest!

The most popular treatments at the hospital during that period were deep insulin and electro-convulsive therapy (ECT or shock treatment as it was usually referred to). The deep insulin patients became easy to spot as they all gained vast amounts of weight – one of the side effects of the treatment – and the shock patients by the dazed and vacant expressions on their faces as they returned from a treatment, and the gradual build-up of fear as the time drew closer to their next one. I was able to avoid both these options and was treated with drugs for depression and insomnia. I think there were two suicide attempts during my stay, and certainly one of them was successful. The hospital building was Victorian, purpose-built to be used for housing the mentally ill during the nineteenth century. Not a lot had changed, I didn't feel, in the attitude of the outside world toward those contained within the sombre walls of institutional 'insanity'. In the early 1960s mental illness was still an unknown and feared quantity as far as most of the general population was concerned, conjuring up images of Bedlam, padded cells, and dribbling, incontinent lunatics destined never to see the light of day again.

The reality was somewhat different: my fellow inmates were not 'mad'. Disturbed? Yes. Depressed? Frequently. Frightened, lonely, lost, unable to deal with the demands of the world in which they found themselves; seeking the comfort of withdrawal into an interior life both literally and metaphysically? Definitely. There was a certain security within those walls: we were all there because of our inability to cope with the 'real' world, and very little was expected of us; the routines of hospital life were soothing; responsibility minimal. The staff were kind; the weaving of baskets and knitting of tea cosies prompted by twice-weekly sessions of occupational therapy calmed our troubled psyches. Visitors appeared unsettled by their proximity to the inmates, and showed a barely concealed longing to escape the discomfort it engendered.

However, all good things must come to an end and, six weeks after I was admitted, I was discharged on the understanding that I would seek psychiatric help on my return to London. I did in fact find a psychiatrist who was willing to treat me; but my father refused to allow it, wanting to foster his belief that my breakdown was an isolated incident which had been treated and would not reoccur, and that further therapy could therefore be of no possible value. My father was totally unready to accept that my emotional condition was far from resolved; to do so would have meant acknowledging his own contribution to my fragile emotional state.

And so I returned to the Academy and the completion of my fifth and penultimate term. As I had missed the first six weeks, John Fernald was kind enough to offer me the chance of retaking the whole term, but I was anxious to enter my sixth and final term and take my chances in the world of professional actors.

My relationship with Tony Hopkins remains the most dominant influence of my RADA years, and it was no secret that he and I were considered the 'most likely to succeed' by our peers. Some years later we found ourselves playing opposite each other in a television play about the life of David Lloyd George. Tony played Lloyd George and I his Polish mistress. After the recording we all congregated in the BBC bar at Television Centre in White City. Tony left before I did; he reached the door, paused, then turned round and came up to me. He held me quite fiercely by my shoulders and said with great urgency, 'Don't you ever give up; you have it in you to become the greatest actress of the twentieth century.' Tony fulfilled the prophecies of our peers; I, alas, did not and it would be many years before I came to realise why I had sabotaged my promising career – in fact, not until I arrived in the African bush some four decades later.

5
Marriage and Movies

During my final term at RADA Tony Hopkins and I were having coffee one evening at the coffee bar just around the corner from the Academy. We were approached by two young men who introduced themselves as James Scott and Drewe Henley; they had a script they had written and wondered if Tony and I would be interested in playing the leading characters. They told us the story, left us both with a copy of the script which we duly read and agreed to play the parts they had in mind for us. James was producing the film – he later went on to win a Best Short Film Oscar – and Drewe, who was also an actor, was going to direct it. I remember very little about the actual film except that it was fun to make and a great learning curve for two young actors eager for their first experience of working on film.

Although my memories of the film itself have been lost in the mists of time, I remember Drewe very clearly. He was seriously beautiful with dark blond hair, blue eyes that actually twinkled and a smile that lit up a room. He was also six feet tall and blessed with the body of a god. He and James shared a large room in Parsons Green which had no bathroom, an outside loo, and a dubious butler's sink which boasted one cold tap and that was it. Cooking was accomplished on a single gas ring. But, despite the lack of conveniences, the room itself radiated charm. The floor was wooden and in my memory so were the walls; the ceiling was arched and supported by beams and the feeling was very French and rather rustic but with a suggestion of sophistication. Drewe smoked Disque Bleu and Gitanes cigarettes which aided the French ambience, wore faded Levis and a leather flying officer's jacket, and looked seriously sexy.

Reader, I married him... How could I fail to fall deeply in love with this beautiful, blue-eyed boy? He was kind and gentle and also deeply in love with me. A match made in heaven, it would appear. Nine months after we met we were married in a Norman church situated in the Surrey countryside. It was December 21st, the day of the winter solstice and the day after my twentieth birthday; a light dusting of snow lay on the ground and caressed the bare branches of the trees with silver that shimmered softly in the shy light from a pale lemon sun. Holly berries kissed with snow sparkled seductively, spiders' webs playing host to Jack Frost flashed ice diamonds, ruby and sapphire, emerald and gold, rich jewel colours that glowed in the fading light as dusk claimed the remainder of the day. So far, so good; but that was the best it got...

Our marriage was doomed from the start, based as it was on our mutual fantasies: Drewe's being that he had married a woman – albeit a very young one – and mine that I had married my Prince and would live happily ever after in a gingerbread cottage in a forest. But far from being an adult, my emotional development had ceased many years earlier; and the repression of the convent combined with the unconscious sexuality that had defined my relationship with my father had resulted in a complete negation of my own sexuality. I had no sexual feelings at all and therefore no sexual response. I was a child in a woman's body, wanting only to be held as a child; my reaction to the sexual act one of terror and pain. As my husband was a virile young man in his sexual prime the omens for a successful union were less than optimistic, the house of cards upon which our union was built destined to collapse at any moment.

That moment came three-and-a-half years later. It was inevitable that Drewe would look elsewhere for the sexual affirmation that I had been unable to provide, and after several liaisons finally decided to leave me for Felicity Kendal and the good life. Although the demise of our marriage was inevitable, it nevertheless proved extremely painful and was the deciding factor in my decision to move to Los Angeles and attempt to establish a life and career in another country, another continent.

Prior to the demise of my marriage, my career had been proving very successful. I left RADA and managed to secure the services of one of the best agents in town: Julian Belfrage, a partner of Terry Plunkett Greene, their offices situated at 110 Jermyn Street. It was 1964 and the air was buzzing with change; everything seemed charged with excitement, the atmosphere was electric, anything and everything appeared possible. Julian was a young man with impossibly blue eyes, dark hair, enormous charm, a public school education and a fondness for the horses. He was also an extremely talented agent, both in acquiring work for his clients and spotting talent at a distance of a hundred yards. When I joined the agency, both Judi Dench and John Hurt were clients and he did extremely well by both of them.

I started off well, going into a 'telly' with John Hurt, Ian McShane and Drewe. At the time of my audition, which was for a part called 'Girl in Café', I was unaware that Drewe had also auditioned for one of the leads. We both got our parts but my fury when I discovered that Drewe was playing one of the leads and I was playing a part that didn't even warrant a name knew no bounds and I have to acknowledge that I was less than charitable in my response to his good fortune. Plates were thrown and feet were stamped and things deteriorated rapidly from there. My behaviour was appalling.

More small parts in tellies followed, then the juvenile lead in a West End play, *The Judge* by John Mortimer (not one of his best), and two films for Hammer: *The Plague of the Zombies* and *The Reptile*. They were good days; I loved the early-morning drive through the quiet and stillness of the Buckinghamshire countryside as we made our way to Bray Studios and my 6.30 make-up call. I found the family atmosphere that permeated the studio extremely seductive, and the kindness shown by the experienced crew toward a young actress, still cutting her teeth where film technique was concerned, such a boon. The atmosphere inside a film studio where a large group of people work as one towards a common goal – the finished film – creates a feeling of great strength, power and energy. The unity experienced by those involved, where 'reel' life assumes far greater importance than 'real' life, is highly charged, intense and totally addictive. That creative impulse was evident at Bray Studios and I treasure the memories of those days.

Of the two films I made for Hammer, both of which have become classics of the genre, I have a particular affection for *Zombies*; the first assistant director, Bert Batt (wonderful name) was extremely good at his job and very kind to me. He left when we began shooting *Reptile* to go on to another picture and although his replacement was equally good at the job, the dynamics of the crew were subtly altered, as always happens when a new element is introduced into any group of people.

At that time in the sixties every young girl seemed to wear her hair long with a fringe, in an attempt to emulate the beautiful model Jean Shrimpton, and I was no exception. I wore it like that in both films although I'm not sure that fringes were at all as ubiquitous in the late nineteenth century as they were in the mid twentieth, but there you go. Poetic licence!

The films were shot back to back and, as anyone who is familiar with both of them will have realised, the exact same set was used for both films. They didn't waste money at Bray Studios. But horror-film fans are very forgiving, and seem – from meetings and discussions I've had with some of them over the years – of the opinion that it added to the charm of the production. I'd never thought of horror movies as having charm, but to those who know their stuff apparently those two did!

I was fortunate in that I found favour with André Morell, who was playing a leading role and was then in his mid fifties although he seemed at least a decade older. He came from, and was a wonderful example of, a completely different school of acting. Lots of one-eyebrow-raised-quizzically acting featured in his performance; although, unlike Roger Moore who also made a speciality of eyebrow acting, I think André was able to raise both eyebrows simultaneously should the part require it. How extraordinary that one can build a successful career and accumulate vast wealth in the process solely because of an ability to raise one eyebrow independently of the other.

I say I was fortunate to find favour with André because our leading lady didn't. He took an intense dislike to her and her interpretation of her character. The venom dripped from him as soon as she appeared on set, and I fully expected his teeth to rot from the acidity of the remarks that issued from his mouth whenever he was required to work with her.

Turning into a zombie was not without its difficulties, however. Apparently the only way to successfully dispatch a zombie – one of the undead – was via beheading. Or certainly for this zombie. This meant I had to have a plaster cast made of my head, which involved a thick layer of plaster of Paris being poured into a mould and attached to my face leaving only my nostrils free to enable me to breathe. As the process was guaranteed to induce claustrophobia and I was seriously claustrophobic in my younger days, I hung on as long as I could but unfortunately cracked minutes before it was due to be removed. So did the mould, so I had to endure the entire process again but managed to do so to the bitter end the second time around.

But even more unpleasant was the make-up I wore as The Reptile. It took hours to apply and involved a great deal of spirit gum, artificial fangs and a mask glued to the upper part of my face. I was unable to eat while I was wearing it and sucked liquids through a straw. The fangs were made by a dentist in Hammersmith who apparently specialised in supplying unusual orthodontics for the film industry. Because removing the make-up and the spirit gum that was used to attach the mask played havoc with my skin, leaving it very sore and blotchy, I had to have a day off after each day I worked to enable my skin to settle down sufficiently to undergo the process once again.

The restaurant at Bray was wonderful as evidenced by my hips as filming continued, until my producer felt compelled to tell me that gaining any more weight was not a good idea, but laying off the sponge pudding (drenched with golden syrup, covered in custard and topped off with cream) was. As he kept a very beady eye on me in the restaurant, I nibbled on grapes, as I longed for the type of metabolism that would enable me to eat anything I desired without gaining an ounce. I loved, and still do, carbs, fat and sugar: a deadly combination, but infinitely pleasurable.

A film called *The Gypsy* followed, later retitled as *Sky West and Crooked*. It was written by Mary Hayley Bell, directed by John Mills and starred their daughter Hayley in the leading role. Ian McShane played opposite her, the gypsy of the original title, and I (also a gypsy) his love interest until he abandoned me for the nubile charms of young Hayley. I enjoyed that film too. Ian was always a delight, both socially and professionally, and we were filming in beautiful countryside – quite where I forget but my memory does retain the scent of summer roses, their petals palest yellow edged with pink, poignant with dew, and chocolate-box cottages emerging from the mists of early morning as the sun rose in the sky and saluted the day. That of course was when it wasn't pissing down and we found ourselves huddling, wet and miserable, under inadequate cover bemoaning our lot with all the vigour at our disposal. Actors, especially wet actors, are capable of surprising vigour.

My career in television continued to flourish; I was starting to gain a reputation and leading roles were offered and accepted. Then at the age of twenty-three I was offered the lead in an international movie: a comedy called *Don't Raise the Bridge, Lower the River*, playing opposite the American comedian Jerry Lewis. I was with Julian in his office a few days after the offer had been made, when he said 'I always had a feeling about you.' We were both thrilled and I was extremely excited. Costume fittings followed and my entire wardrobe designed by a talented designer by the name of Maxine Leighton. My resemblance to Audrey Hepburn was quite pronounced in those days and my wardrobe reflected that. Harry Frampton was my make-up artist, a man of great personal style and elegance. The omens were good.

The film was being directed by an American called Jerry Paris, a delightful man who radiated good humour and warmth. His job was a difficult one, as prior to this production Jerry Lewis had written, produced, directed and starred in most of his previous movies and was reluctant to relinquish control of this one. He also had his current mistress with him and in order to preserve his image as a happily married man, devoted to his family, he took it into his head to fly back to LA after work finished one Friday evening, and staggered jet-lagged and rather the worse for wear into the studio the following Monday morning. He'd also managed to find time for a haircut and, as we were finishing up a scene we had started shooting on the Friday, his changed appearance threw continuity into a slight tizz. Unfortunately he hadn't found time to learn his lines, so shooting was frequently interrupted by his inability to remember them.

Finally such was his frustration that he threw his arms up in the air, turned to the director and said, 'The girl doesn't know her lines,' and went to walk off the set.

'Mr Lewis,' I called (in quite a demanding tone of voice, I have to admit), 'my name is Jacqueline Pearce and as we are to be working together for a further eight weeks, I would appreciate it if you would have the courtesy to remember it. I *do* know my lines; it is you who does not. I shall now go to my dressing room, and when you are ready to make me an apology, I shall be ready to receive it.' So I did, and he did, and if harmony wasn't exactly restored – he exhibited a certain *froideur* towards me for the remainder of the shoot – we were at least able to work together as professionals.

While we were filming, Sammy Davis Jr and Peter Lawford were working on the next sound stage making a film called *Salt and Pepper*. They of course knew the two Jerrys and frequently joined us for lunch in the studio restaurant. Lawford didn't thrill me, but I warmed totally to Sammy. He was warm, witty, full of exuberant energy and great kindness, and I began to see him after work when he entertained friends in his suite at – I think it was – the Hilton hotel. All the great and good of the day seemed to gather in Sammy's suite; Leslie Bricusse and his wife Evie were frequent visitors, and beautiful blonde girls with miniskirts and great legs were always in abundance. He would take us to dinner at the White Elephant restaurant which was situated on the banks of the Thames, or to fashionable Italian restaurants on the King's Road, and was always ready to party until dawn.

I always left these gatherings early unless I wasn't called for the next day's filming, but over a period of time realised that Sammy's big fear was being alone. He surrounded himself with people from dawn to dusk, always delaying the moment when the last guest would depart, leaving him alone with himself and the demons that appeared to haunt him. He was a man of great sensitivity and vulnerability who had achieved so much against tremendous odds.

FROM BYFLEET TO THE BUSH

One night he took me to dinner alone; just him and me, no one else. This was a huge departure from the norm for Sammy, something he very rarely did, as he confirmed for me during our conversation. He told me that I had become extremely important to him; he found my lack of worldliness and extreme naivety very appealing, and knew that he was falling in love with me.

I was still married to Drewe and Sam was married to the Swedish actress May Britt, although both our unions were edging perilously close to the rocks. In many ways we were kindred spirits and found great consolation in each other's company. Was I in love with Sam? I certainly loved him but was incapable of a complete relationship with any man, although I did try!

One night he took me to the studio where he was recording some songs; one of them, *Something in Your Smile*, he dedicated to me. It was heady stuff indeed for a convent girl, with very little life experience and an overwhelming need to be loved. It was that need for love which motivated my desire to be an actress. Surely if I proved myself to be successful I would be worthy of the love and acceptance I craved? I had no self-esteem, self-awareness or self-knowledge. In fact I didn't have a clue who I really was and acting provided me with the opportunity to escape from the bonds of self; to immerse myself in someone else's reality. Many years later in a session with my psychiatrist, when asked what it was I wanted out of life, my reply was: 'To have the whole world love me.'

One of my abiding memories of Sam is that despite his hefty consumption of bourbon and his habit of chain-smoking his way through countless packs of Dunhill cigarettes and only ever getting a minimal amount of sleep, he would wake each morning with the sweetest breath I have ever encountered, before or since. Some achievement!

My friendship with Sam continued for many years – he would always call me when he was in London – and I recall one occasion very clearly. We hadn't seen each other for some months when he called me and invited me to come on over to the Playboy Club where he was currently staying. I assumed we would be having a quiet night in catching up with each other's news. I refused his offer of a car and said I would make my own way there. I left my flat wearing a new yellow dress – especially bought for the occasion – and decided to walk the short distance to the Playboy Club. I was half way through my journey when the heavens opened and every taxi seemed to have disappeared off the planet. My dress, which was made of some man-made material, proceeded to shrink drastically, and the hem which was at a discreet height just above the knee at the start of my journey now clung to the tops of my thighs. My false eyelashes uncurled, unglued and dripped mascara in several rivulets down my flushed face. I arrived hot, sweating and in no way prepared for the evening which lay ahead. It transpired that we weren't staying in after all, but going out to dinner with friends!

I got into a car and did my best to tug my dress back to a respectable length, reglued my eyelashes and rubbed off the offending rivulets of mascara, but still looked like shite at the end of it. We drove to a quiet part of the Thames and there in its centre lay a large boat. 'Oh!' I said to Sam, 'what a lovely idea, a restaurant on a boat!' We were rowed out to the boat, which turned out to be not a boat at all but a very grand yacht. We were piped aboard by men in what appeared to be full naval regalia, and arrived at the top of the gangplank to be greeted by our hosts: Elizabeth Taylor and Richard Burton.

Still tugging at my skirt and wishing that the ground would open up and swallow me we joined our fellow guest, the director Joseph Losey, in the salon. La Taylor was resplendent in a purple kimono with matching turban, the sparkles from her diamonds dazzling to behold, the most splendid being the ring she wore on her right hand. It was *the* diamond, the one Burton had lavished half a million pounds or thereabouts on. It was the size of a pigeon's egg and spectacularly vulgar. I couldn't take my eyes off it, so mesmerised was I by this rock which could have solved the financial problems of several third-world countries. What opulence! How did anyone manage to accrue the vast amounts of money required for such a purchase? We had dinner and I listened to the conversation taking place around me, but was unable to contribute anything myself. It was an awe-inspiring evening for a twenty-four-year-old completely out of her depth.

'You're very quiet,' said Burton suddenly, 'what's going on in that pretty little head?' All eyes turned towards me, La Taylor's glittering ominously. I muttered something, stammering incoherently and prayed to a God I didn't believe in to make me disappear. When we finally left it was raining again, and Elizabeth was kind enough to lend me one of her mink coats to provide protection from the elements as we were rowed back to the shore. She also instructed the boat man to collect it on arrival.

The last contact I had with Sam was many years later when I telephoned him from a hospital for the mentally disturbed in Pasadena. He refused to take my call. After so many years of friendship it was a sad ending to our relationship but also totally understandable. I learned of his death from throat cancer some years later and grieved for a kind, gentle, hugely talented man who had given me so much over the years. RIP Sam, RIP.

By 1967 my marriage to Drewe was over; but just before it ended I was able to buy the house we had been renting in Richmond. My salary for *Don't Raise the Bridge* had been £2,000. I bought the house for £1,250 so still had change with which to effect some essential repairs. It was a three-storey house, with sitting tenants in the basement – the main reason for its low price – but shortly after I purchased it they decided to move out. So at the age of twenty-three I was the owner of my own fully paid-up home, with a career promising great success ahead of me: the world it seemed was indeed my oyster. So why do I now find myself penniless, virtually homeless, seriously unemployed and with all my wordly possessions capable of fitting into several black rubbish bags? Why did I forsake the infinite rewards of 'reel' life for the bleakness and difficulties of 'real' life? Good questions...

My fall from grace wasn't intentional but merely the result of an acute lack of financial reality, a gullible personality, an omission to contemplate the future and what it may contain and a lack of common sense so great that it constituted a severe handicap. I decided after Drewe's departure to sell the house and move into a flat nearer to central London. The house contained too many memories to make remaining there viable; I wanted a fresh start in new surroundings and this I achieved. But... what I should have done was rent out the house, thus maintaining my investment, and used the rental money to pay for a flat. Ain't hindsight great?! What I in fact did was sell the house for £1,600, give half to Drewe – even though he had nothing to do with its purchase – and begin my new life assetless in a flat in Queensway for a rent of eighteen pounds a week and with a few hundred pounds in my pocket.

The flat was in a mansion block over the Queensway skating rink and within spitting distance of Hyde Park. Drewe and I had acquired a cairn terrier named Tammy who was my pride and joy and remained with me after the break-up. Tam was infinitely loveable and the greatest of comforts during the sadness that haunted me for so long after the pain of divorce. We would go for long walks in the park, and watching him snuffle around in the bushes and hare off after any Great Dane or Alsatian that took his fancy was a source of endless delight. He was a great theatre dog and I would take him to rehearsals where he would tuck himself tidily under a chair or table, only appearing when summoned, or remain quietly in the dressing room while I was recording in the studio with never a bark or a growl to disturb those around him. That of course would be unthinkable during these days of rigid Health and Safety rules.

But my new surroundings failed to provide relief from the pain of loss, so after deciding that London was not large enough to contain Drewe, his new amour Felicity and myself, I decided to seek pastures new in a faraway land and booked my passage to America. This proved to be my second Big Mistake.

6
Hollywood

I left Tammy with my father and stepmother; they lived in the country and would, I felt sure, provide him with the life of Riley to which he had become accustomed. I was taken to the airport by the family who were en route to their annual two-week holiday in Cornwall. Travelling was still an adventure in those days and it was unthinkable to travel without taking great care to be suitably 'booted and suited', or in my case gloved and hatted, for the journey. I settled into my economy-class seat, and contemplated the uncertain future that lay ahead of me.

The fact that no one could be less suited than I to a life in Hollywood had never crossed my mind. I had no plan: no idea how to establish myself in a foreign country, let alone how to obtain work. I've always been brilliant at making life-or-death decisions due to never thinking things through; never asking myself the practical questions that should have informed my decisions. I simply 'decided and did', the enormous pitfalls engendered by those ill-informed decisions only making themselves apparent when I had fallen head first into the many and varied pits that inevitably made themselves known to me as I continued on my journey into unchartered waters.

I was met at LA airport by Sammy's personal assistant Jim Waters, taken to his modest house on the outskirts of Beverly

Hills, introduced to his wife Luddy, and told I had been booked into the Sunset Plaza Motel on the famous Sunset Strip and would be taken there after we had enjoyed a night out at The Factory, a recently opened nightclub that Sam had shares in. I received this news with some dismay, never having been a party girl, and after having spent what felt like several decades in the air courtesy of Pan American wanted nothing but a hot bath and a comfortable bed. My feeble requests for this finale to a very long day were met with adamant refusals and I was dragged, wretched with exhaustion, to the nightclub with all that that involved: loud music and banks of coloured lights playing over the crowded dance floor and flickering disconcertingly over the faces of the revellers, turning them electric blue, pink, yellow – indeed all the colours of the rainbow, which should have looked attractive but somehow managed to achieve a slightly sinister effect.

I've always disliked crowded places, music so loud that conversation is impossible: it is a barrier to intimacy and creates – in me certainly – a sense of alienation and isolation that disturbs and confuses me. I felt sorry for the waiters, who were unemployed actors and had to fight their way through a packed crowd, weighed down with an assortment of Californian cocktails sporting tiny umbrellas atop a glass containing glacé cherries both red and green, enough fresh fruit to fulfil one's 'five a day' requirements and several ounces of alcohol. My dislike of parties and nightclubs was an obvious hindrance to developing my social life and meeting possible future employers, as a great deal of business was done at these gatherings. I loved the work itself, but completely lacked the temperament to pursue the networking side of obtaining it.

We finally stumbled out of The Factory at around two a.m., the rest of the party extremely merry and distinctly the worse for wear. Still being a teetotaller and remaining one until I saw the light at the age of thirty-five I was uncompromisingly sober, nerve ends shrieking for the oblivion of sleep and some privacy. I was finally deposited at the Sunset Plaza where I staggered into the suite that Sam had thoughtfully arranged for me, collapsed onto the most enormous bed I had ever seen and surrendered myself to the embrace of healing sleep.

During the next few days while I remained at the Plaza I explored my surroundings. I was on Sunset Strip and it was just like the movies! I found it incredibly exciting; the bill boards were enormous, the faces shining out of them glittering with glamour, exotic with allure and the suggestion of secrets to share. I longed to be among their number; to reach the pinnacle of success that would enable me to achieve the love and recognition I craved.

The size of everything made me feel like Alice in Wonderland. I went to a restaurant for dinner and ordered a steak and salad; when it arrived the steak was so enormous that it could easily have fed a family of four for a fortnight, the salad containing half the vegetables of a modest-sized English allotment – an awesome sight. I gazed at my plate, fascinated by this, my first experience of American excess; memories of the rationing which held England in its frugal grip until the mid fifties and had made an indelible impression on me were less than a decade away. What serious opulence, what divine decadence! I surreptitiously observed my fellow diners, and saw plates as full as mine; desserts served in dishes the size of canoes, filled with a large assortment of ice creams in heady colours – the soft green of pistachio, the rich blue-black of blueberries, crystallised fruit, nuts, sprinkles and marshmallows drenched in hot fudge sauce.

I left the Plaza a week later after a fruitless search for an apartment. I wanted to live in the Hollywood Hills situated way above the Strip. I had been driven there by Luddy and found it inhabited mainly by the artistic as opposed to the movie community; the houses striking in their individuality, radiating charm, painted in gypsy colours and displaying gardens planted with herbs, vegetables and big, green bushes that were in evidence everywhere. I discovered later that they were marijuana plants and smoking 'pot' a regular activity in the life of the community. But it proved impossible for me to live there; a car was essential and my inability to drive the stumbling block that denied me access to this eclectic group of free spirits.

And so it was that I ended up in an apartment off Sunset Strip, housed in a block on North Palm. It was anonymous and extremely ugly, the concrete walls having been coated with something that created a stucco effect. The main room had a galley kitchen and the cupboards were made of pretend wood as were the worktop and breakfast bar. The floor was covered in a cheap green-and-brown carpet that would have benefited from a thorough shampooing; the windows were small and let in minimal daylight. I'm sure it was representative of many apartments in Hollywood: soulless, anonymous and emitting the despair of broken dreams and the loss of hope. I hated it! What on earth was I doing there? I seemed to have very little option – I was in a foreign country and unfamiliar with the terrain, had very little money and was reluctant to lean too heavily on the few acquaintances I had, recognising that they had their own, very busy lives and would soon lose interest in the problems posed by an insecure, needy addition to their midst.

Driving lessons followed and it soon became obvious that I was not a natural born driver. I was never confident behind the wheel, got my first ticket a week after I scraped through my test and remained a road menace during the three years I lived in Los Angeles. My biggest transgression occurred a couple of years later when I was returning from the Valley to Santa Monica: it was rush hour, I never enjoyed travelling on the freeway at the best of times and in my anxiety took the exit as opposed to the entry ramp... The enormity of my mistake hit me as I suddenly found myself confronted by six lanes of traffic screeching to a halt. I tried frantically to turn the car around, heart racing as my blood pressure soared and sweat slid copiously down my face, its salty sting as it hit my eyes rendering sight difficult as I banged into the concrete barriers and tried to ignore the looks of horror and astonishment on the faces of the occupants of the cars whose exit I blocked. I finally managed to get the car facing in the right direction, exited the freeway, pulled over to the side of the road where I proved an easy target for the torrents of (totally justified) abuse that were hurled at me from the drivers of the cars I had obstructed, and waited for the panic to subside.

I rented a Mustang which I kept reasonably damage-free, and joined the Actors Studio West as an observer. The Actors Studio had been founded in New York by Lee Strasberg, but due to the vast number of actors living on the west coast had opened another branch in LA. In order to become a member one had to audition in front of Strasberg, which I duly did, passed and was accepted as a fully fledged member. I took pride in this achievement having been awed by the work of some of the members who had appeared in films: Marlon Brando, Montgomery Clift, Rod Steiger and Karl Malden to name but a few. But I found the seminars which Strasberg gave, when he came out west pretty much incomprehensible. That's not to say they weren't full of wisdom and illumination for those with ears to hear; my own failure to glean any useful information was doubtless due to my inability to absorb them. But it did provide me with the opportunity to work on scenes with other actors, observe them at work and absorb, perhaps through some kind of osmosis, an awareness of another approach to the work. It also enabled me to keep my hand in and hang on to my identity as an actress. Very important as I had no other; if I wasn't an actress, then what was I? I wasn't yet ready to face the reality: that I was a sad, alienated child living with wounds too savage to heal, too deep to sustain, blindly searching for identity and wholeness, for a place of safety in a world I found too harsh, too painful to endure.

I saw very little of Sammy during this period – he was constantly out of town, working in clubs in Las Vegas, Reno and New York, when he wasn't occupied abroad – but he had paid my rent and leased the Mustang for me. He had offices in the 9000 Building on the Strip, and one day I was summoned to a meeting with his business partner, Sy Marsh. Sy was a relatively new addition to Sammy's staff; he had previously been an agent of many years' standing with, I believe, the William Morris Agency. Now, anyone with even a modicum of nous would have made sure she left that meeting with interviews with agents lined up, and offers of introduction to the great and good of the Hollywood hierarchy. As I wouldn't recognise an opportunity if it was staring me in the face (it was), what I in fact did was accept the position of receptionist and answerer of Sammy's fan mail, which enabled me to support myself and live financially independent of Sam.

And so I began my career as receptionist for 'Sammy Davis Enterprises, Sy March Ltd', which was how I had to introduce myself every time I answered the constantly ringing telephones. So, far from advancing my own career as an actress, I made calls on Sy's behalf to producers and directors as he set up appointments for other young actresses who had caught his eye and spent hours with him in his locked office, presumably discussing their careers. We never discussed mine.

Being unused to a nine-to-five routine, and being a night person by both temperament and inclination, I resorted to what appeared to be the drug of choice on both sides of the Atlantic: black bombers. These were ostensibly prescribed as appetite suppressants and did a brilliant job of not only suppressing the appetite but of supplying seemingly endless amounts of energy: 'uppers', *par excellence*. I would fall into bed around three or four a.m. and emerge bleary-eyed and shell-shocked at seven-thirty in order to prepare myself for yet another stimulating day as a receptionist. I ceased to be an actress in the eyes of those around me and became just another 'out-of-towner' swelling the ranks of the aspiring starlets who flocked to Hollywood looking for the 'break' that never materialised.

When I was still very new in town, I was advised by a fellow actress that it was imperative that I subscribe to a telephone answering service, which I instantly did. After several weeks without receiving any messages, my embarrassment began to increase so I hit on the idea of calling myself and leaving messages using an assortment of accents to disguise my identity. I'm still not sure to this day if the operators saw through my little ruse or if I did convince them that I was an extremely popular and industrious lady. I cancelled the service eventually, being increasingly uncomfortable with the deception.

The same actress told me one day that she had just joined OA – Overeaters Anonymous – and thought it might be a good idea if I did the same. Always anxious to please, I joined and immediately became a compulsive overeater, making frequent nocturnal trips to the 24-hour grocery store at the end of my block and returning with brown paper sacks groaning with ice cream, marshmallow topping, countless candy bars and cream cakes. I obviously had a talent for compulsive overeating, gaining twenty pounds effortlessly in a matter of weeks despite my best efforts to curtail my food intake. But the black bombers provided little protection against the hunger that consumed me; the craving that food could never sate, but which was the manifestation of the spiritual hunger for integration that was to torment me for many years.

It never crossed my mind that I had a choice in the way I lived my life. It never occurred to me to return to London and resume my career. I continued living in my concrete cell, combining the morning black bombers with night-time sleeping pills, diligently answering Sammy's phones, finding consolation at the Actors Studio and giving my body to an endless parade of men with the tacit understanding that they would hold me and, for a short time at least, I could cling to the illusion of warmth, safety and protection. I had never experienced that depth of loneliness before; it paralysed me and rendered me numb. Tears are blurring my vision as I write, as memories of those lost years come flooding back; as I view from the vantage point of maturity the pain, sadness and despair that was to haunt that child/woman for so many more years to come. And she had no idea.

Eventually I moved from my concrete cell into the first of many apartments, establishing the peripatetic lifestyle which has dominated my life ever since. I yearned for a home: for the security, warmth and safety it suggested; somewhere I could feel protected, loved and wanted. I had yet to understand and accept that everything I sought, with ever increasing desperation, lay in the deep recesses of my shattered psyche. I wasn't going to be 'rescued'; I wasn't going to 'find myself in another'. I was going to have to heal myself, learn to become my own mother, nurture the damaged child crying ceaselessly within me, become my own strength and protector; achieve my own integration.

And then I made a friend! We met at an acting class we both attended: his name was Bob Greenough, he was an actor (natch, this being Hollywood) but worked as a mailman for the Beverly Hills post office. He introduced himself as a farm boy from Illinois, glowing with the good health and perfect teeth evident in so many Americans. Bob was twenty-seven, blond, blue-eyed, tall and very good-looking. He was also gay and shared a house with his lover Hartje who originally hailed from Germany and was referred to by Bob as 'der Fuhrer'. They lived in Santa Monica and it wasn't long before I moved out of yet another concrete cell and into their spare room. The house was charming: light, airy and seconds from the beach. Life was looking up big time. Bob and Hartje provided me with a home, companionship and wonderful friendship. I delighted in Santa Monica, and spent hours drinking coffee at outdoor cafés, watching the world go by.

I knew the time had come to leave 'Sammy Davis Enterprises, Sy Marsh Ltd'; I wanted my days free which would enable me to work at the Studio, practise my craft and be around fellow thespians. Try as I might, I was unable to adapt to the nine-to-five routine of office life; and the cycle of uppers and downers was now an established part of my daily routine. I left with no regrets, breathed a huge sigh of relief as I regained some of my identity as an actress, and sought evening employment in the twilight world of the cocktail waitress.

My first gig in my new role was at a bar in Santa Monica. Not being a drinker myself I was unfamiliar with the multitude of cocktails advertised on the bar's menus. Alfie, the English bartender, would mix the drinks as I called them out, place them on my tray and leave me to present them to the appropriate table. Not being able to distinguish between them, I would hold up each glass, smile imploringly and hope that the correct customer claimed the correct cocktail. This usually worked so I was able to stumble my way through each shift without too many mishaps.

The bar was in the basement of a hotel, and after my shift had finished at two a.m. I found myself one early morning in the room of one of the guests. Clothes had been shed and coupling achieved, when suddenly the earth moved. This was not a symptom of the sexual ecstasy I had long sought, but due rather to the earthquake, 6.5 on the Richter scale, that was grumbling beneath us. Coitus was well and truly interruptus by the furniture sliding to the other side of the room. 'Earthquake,' said my host, 'gotta get outta here.'

I hastily reapplied my lipstick, slipped into my high heels, and followed him out into the hallway. We weaved our way down several flights of stairs as the building continued to sway ominously and eventually found our way to reception, the exit and the gathering crowd of fellow guests grouped around the swimming pool which was sloshing its contents over the sides as the earth continued to move beneath us. Clad as I was in nothing but my lipstick and high heels, a sensitive soul wrapped a towel around my exposed body as the tremors finally shuddered to a halt and the resultant damage was surveyed by the shocked group of survivors. Trees had been wrested from the earth that housed them, their exposed roots like giant claws in the gaping craters, tables and chairs lay in ungainly heaps, huge cracks had appeared in the walls of the building and the broken glass from the windows lay glinting on the ground like crystals in the early morning light. Santa Monica was lucky; the freeway was still waiting for the early-morning rush hour which would commence just thirty minutes later, so the loss of life was minimal compared to the carnage that would have been created had the freeways been crowded.

I managed to make my way home – still dressed in the towel – and after lots of TLC from Bob and der Fuhrer reflected on my good fortune in having survived the experience – and the need for another 'gig' as repairs to the hotel would make it unoperational for some time.

I found another position as a cocktail waitress in a strip club on La Cienega Boulevard. The waitresses weren't required to shed their clothes, only the girls who performed their routines to canned music, their surgically enhanced breasts defying gravity and their attitudes of profound boredom not conducive to the eroticism demanded by the owner of the club.

We waitresses wore black tights with leotards and – in the case of the other girls – black high-heeled shoes. I found high heels too uncomfortable to wear for an eight-hour shift, so wore the flat-heeled character shoes that had remained a permanent feature of my wardrobe since my RADA days. I was a bit of a disaster actually, the whole purpose of my job being to sell as many drinks as possible called 'overs'. The club had a policy of a two-drink minimum requirement. This meant that any drinks sold over the minimum were classed as 'overs'; and the more 'overs' we sold, the more the management beamed beatifically upon us, and their pleasure was reflected in the bonuses that accompanied the meagre minimum wage that was our basic pay. If I managed to make one 'over' per night I was lucky, but the other girls sold vast amounts and eventually I asked to be told their secret. 'Well,' said Carole, who was twenty years old and already on her second marriage, 'it sure would help if you'd stop wearin' those trick-or-treat shoes, slap on some more make-up and flirt with the guys fer Chrissakes. And if that don't work, tell 'em ya got three kids under five, yer ol' man ran out on ya, and the owner'll fire ya if you can't sell more liquor. Hustle 'em honey, that's what I do and it sure does work like a charm. You try it and see if it don't.'

I pondered this advice for some time but was unable to put it into practice; my feet rebelled against the confinement of high heels and my conscience against the subterfuge required to part the men from their money. So I continued to clump around the club in my 'trick-or-treat' character shoes, contributing very little to the finances of the club, until I was relieved of my responsibilities by a hostile manager who informed me rather brusquely that he'd had 'great hopes for you kid, but you didn't deliver hon; you sure didn't deliver.' So I bade my farewell to the club, the name of which was The Losers. The irony escaped me for many years…

By this time I had moved in with my host of earthquake night. He designed guitars and thought he might successfully ply his trade in London, so at his suggestion we decided to leave LA and see what London had to offer. But for that, I may well have remained in Hollywood indefinitely, so for enabling me to leave I have to thank him. My attempts to establish myself in Hollywood were less than the success story I had hoped for! True, I now knew the difference between a Tom Collins and a Singapore Sling, I was a member of the Actors Studio, had made two good friends and met Neil Diamond (a friend of Guitar Man). I was also overweight, frigid (still), frightened, completely lost and without a clue as to who I was. Nil self-knowledge and mega insecurity.

I have of course asked myself what would have happened if I hadn't gone to Hollywood, but had stayed in London and continued with my burgeoning career. I can't know the answer to that question; I can only speculate as to what might have been. If my career had indeed taken off big time, and I had achieved the success and recognition I craved which I was convinced would result in the love and acceptance I believed to be essential for my survival, one thing I can be sure of. Far from resolving my anguish and providing the solution to my massive insecurity, I would have discovered the flaws inherent in fame: the illusion of love, the mirage of acceptance; and when I faced those impostors and saw my dream of release from the pain of separation slipping like sand through my outstretched hands, so great would have been my feelings of betrayal and abandonment that I would have submitted to the insanity that hovered always at my shoulder, and retreated into a darkness that would overwhelm and consume me, and from which I would never emerge. My Hollywood years may have been lost years fraught with difficulties, humiliations and rejections, but at least I was still alive and with a tenuous hold on my sanity, which I doubt would have been the case had I remained in London. So: every cloud...

7
Ups and Downs

Although I returned to England with Guitar Man, that relationship soon went the way of so many others. I found him selfish, immature and unwilling to assume any kind of fiscal responsibility. He was in his late thirties at the time, had been married and fathered five children. His two oldest sons, boys in their mid teens, were sent to join us by their mother and it soon became clear that Guitar Man expected my father to provide for him and his sons. Even if my father had been a millionaire instead of a man of very modest means there is no way he would have fulfilled Guitar Man's expectations; my father believed that men were intended to protect and provide and would frown upon a man who failed to do his duty.

In order to accommodate the boys we had moved to the country and rented a sixteenth-century farmhouse in Edenbridge in Kent. It was Grade 1 Listed and a quite magnificent example of the architecture of the time. I fell in love with it immediately. The main room ran the width of the house; it was the size of a ballroom, had panelled walls and beamed ceilings, a very impressive fireplace at one end and a timbered staircase leading to the upper floor at the other. All the rooms had dark oak beams, there were fireplaces in every room, the furnishings were of the period, the windows were diamond-paned and latticed with lead. My romantic nature was working overtime as I imagined tea and crumpets while sitting around a roaring log fire, the kitchen filled with the aromas of the freshly baked bread I had removed from the Aga (and had of course baked myself) and the rich French coffee which I would serve for breakfast. It was the house of my dreams; it was also mid winter and colder than a witch's tit.

We were supposedly living off money which had been advanced to Guitar Man in return for his design for a new guitar. However, most of it went on the MG two-seater sports car to which he treated himself, so some royalty cheques I had received from the agency were a great boon. I stocked up with coal for the Aga, which I named Agatha and which supplied us with hot water. She was extremely temperamental and very small, having only two hotplates and one oven, and frequently died in the night; having to coax her into life and light again in the freezing cold of a bleak winter morning – a long, arduous and frustrating process only ever undertaken by myself – was not a lot of fun. We did come to understand each other eventually and although she teased me sometimes by pretending to have expired, a thorough rake among the ominous grey ashes would reveal a bed of glowing red coals which I quickly topped up with fresh supplies, groaning with gratitude as I did so.

Along with his other virtues, Guitar Man was also a shining example of a male chauvinist pig. He would drive me into the village and drop me off at the supermarket where I would shop for a 'family' of four which contained three males with extremely large appetites to satisfy. I would stagger out a couple of hours later, laden down with my multitude of purchases and wait for Guitar Man to collect me. He would spend the time waiting for me in the warmth of the local 'caff', playing the pinball machine and the juke box. Bless...

Just as the money ran out, I was cast in a telly and my salary couldn't have been more welcome. We ran out of coal and by the time we could afford to get more, the coalman had run out of supplies. And the house had proved to be less than comfortable; furniture of the period was all well and good, but all the chairs had hard, straight backs; there was nowhere to sit and relax, roaring fires were out of the question without the coal to feed them, the temperature was well below zero and I was not a happy bunny. I knew I would have to leave.

Guitar Man used to go away quite frequently, and I chose one of those occasions to slip away; I've always avoided confrontation whenever possible and was also aware that my absence would make not the slightest bit of difference to Guitar Man's life. I told the boys who quite understood my decision to leave – indeed couldn't understand why I hadn't made it months earlier – and made my way to London without a clue as to what I was going to do next.

After staying with a friend for a few weeks, I found a small flat to rent in Battersea; it was furnished and the rent was affordable. I got a job as a waitress in a fast-food restaurant on the King's Road in Chelsea. The hours were long, the work was demanding, the pay was a joke and my feet hurt like hell! But I was surviving, although my depressive episodes were becoming more frequent and taking their toll on both my physical and emotional health.

Wanting to find a solution to my situation, I decided to explore the benefits of meditation which I understood to be a recipe for mental health and equilibrium. To this end I was initiated into the practice of Transcendental Meditation. After practising diligently for a month, I felt no different than I had before I started. So I returned to the TM Centre to voice my complaint and ask for my money back. I discussed my feelings with a young man who was himself a teacher of the practice and, although I didn't get my money back, he did enable me to understand that a great deal more practice was required on my part before I would reap the undoubted benefits that meditation had to offer. His name was David – although for some reason I always called him Fred; he was three years younger than me; and nine months later I married him. My second marriage was a repeat of my first, ended sixteen months later and was definitely an example of the triumph of hope over experience. When we parted, Fred said to me, 'If ever you decide to write your autobiography, if I feature at all it will be as a footnote.' There was absolutely no animosity in his statement – we had been friends and parted as such, we made each other laugh and liked each other as people – he was simply acknowledging that our time together had been brief and if I ever did pen my autobiography I would be of an age when our short history together would be a soft-focus memory to be replaced by other more vivid chapters of my life.

I moved out of the house we shared in Fulham and into the flat that Fred had found for me on the top floor of a house in a beautiful eighteenth-century terrace on the Old Brompton Road. It was an attic flat with dormer windows, low sloped ceilings and fireplaces. I loved it and the fact that it was also rent-controlled was a huge bonus. Along with a great many others, I gave the landlord's agents the ten per cent deposit they requested, except I upped my deposit to twenty-five per cent which swallowed up most of my available money. I did so because I believed it would convey the seriousness of my desire to obtain the flat and would hopefully aid my cause. I heard nothing for some weeks until I received a letter from the official receiver informing me that the company responsible for leasing the property had been declared bankrupt and inviting me to a meeting with the other schmucks who had also lost their money. It was not a happy gathering and the likelihood of any of us getting our money back was slim to nil. What to do? I fled to the agents to see if I could glean any more information from them. What would happen to the flat? Surely it would still be available for rent?

I was ushered into the office of the gentleman in charge of the property. He told me that the flat would not be rented out until the official receiver had completed his enquiries which would doubtless span many months.

'But what about the £1,250 deposit I gave you? Surely you can return that so I have money available to pay for another flat?'

He regretted that this was not possible and suggested I write to the head of his company who may be able to suggest accommodation in another area. He left the office to find the necessary paperwork; and hanging on a board behind his chair was a set of keys. The label gave the address of the flat under discussion. Without registering what I was doing, I grabbed the keys from the board and secreted them in my handbag. I had just done so when the gentleman returned to the office. He resumed his seat and we looked at each other across his desk. He seemed slightly puzzled as he focused on the red-faced, sweating woman seated opposite him. The enormity of what I had just done had hit me; my heart was thudding in my chest at a rate of knots and black spots were dancing dizzily before my eyes.

'I've just done something rather naughty,' I said.

'Really,' he responded, rather patronisingly I thought.

'Yes,' I replied. 'I saw the keys to the flat on the board behind you, and took the liberty of removing them and transferring them to my handbag.'

He jerked his head around and saw the empty space on the board. 'You can't do that!' he spluttered as his face became suffused with a rather alarming shade of purple. 'I must insist that you hand them back immediately.'

'Certainly,' I agreed. 'You return my cheque for £1,250 and I'll return your keys.'

'I'm not in a position to do that,' he responded.

'Then I have very little option but to retain the keys and move into the flat, because without the means to pay for another, I shall undoubtedly be homeless; a situation I wish to avoid, and as the fuck-up is not of my making I fail to see why I should be expected to pay for it.'

I was amazed by my audacity; a similar audacity to that which had enabled me to speak to Jerry Lewis the way I did. I had always avoided confrontation and had very little idea how to assert myself, but I understood later that there were two areas where my need to assert myself was greater than my fear of being rejected. Those areas were my professionalism and my home. I had refused to allow Jerry Lewis to make me the scapegoat for his own lack of professionalism, as being professional was of paramount importance to me; and the need to find a secure roof over my head, a place of safety where I would find sanctuary and peace was of equal importance. And I needed to work to earn the money to pay for it.

And so I moved into my flat! I had no idea of the legality or otherwise of my actions and expected daily to receive lawyers' letters insisting that I leave the flat immediately, or summonses demanding my presence in court. I questioned whether I would be able to survive jail if my crime proved to justify a prison sentence, and generally lived in a state of high anxiety for some considerable time. But, nothing happened. I discovered who the new agents were, went to see them, made arrangements for the rent to be paid each month, heaved a humongous sigh of relief and thanked my lucky stars that I had finally found a secure roof over my head at a rent that presented no problem, in a flat that I loved, in a part of London that gave me enormous pleasure. Sorted! Ah...

It was around this time that I made the final catastrophic decision as far as my career was concerned. The idea of leaving Julian had never entered my head; he was a wonderful agent who welcomed me back from Hollywood with open arms and I simply assumed that he would remain my agent for all time. I was also very fond of him. But leave him I did and it was downhill all the way from there on. I left because I was (a) seriously thick, (b) gullible to the point of stupidity, (c) incapable of independent thought and (d) as always, desperate to please. So when a recent employee of his (recent due to a parting of the ways) and someone I thought of as a friend told me that Julian was completely wrong for me, didn't have time for me or the necessary enthusiasm, and I would be better off elsewhere, it never occurred to me to question her motives or compare my own experience of Julian with the attitude of the man she was describing. I believed everything she told me – I never doubted that absolutely everyone knew better than me – and pleased her very much by leaving the best agent in town and signing with the rather inferior agency she recommended.

During my marriage to Fred, my depressions and mood swings became more and more pronounced until eventually I consulted my doctor, convinced I had a brain tumour. When I asked him to refer me to a neurologist, he said that he didn't think a neurologist was necessary, but he could recommend an excellent psychiatrist. My luck was in, for Hop, as I always called him, proved to be an extremely talented psychiatrist and my relationship with him one of the most productive of my life.

I first visited his practice in Wimpole Street at the age of twenty-nine and saw him regularly twice a week – three times if I was going through a particularly rough patch – for about seven years; thereafter I cut down to once a week. Hop was a Jungian analyst and exactly what I needed. I could cry on his shoulder, hug him and receive the parental warmth I had always yearned for. He would watch my television appearances and come to see me in the theatre although both mediums were employing me less frequently. Some years later, I decided to go on a course to become a psychodrama therapist. Everyone in the group was psycho and I the only drama! Most of them were in analysis themselves, it being a requirement for therapists in training. They were all Freudians and I would regale them with tales of my Jungian experience which couldn't have been more opposite. One day I was approached by a woman called Sophie. In the course of her work she was going to have to do some public speaking, the thought of which filled her with horror. She wondered if I may be able to assist her in some way. So we agreed that she would come to my flat one evening each week and I would help her with some voice production. After each session we'd chat over a cup of coffee and discuss how our own therapy was progressing. Sophie was really quite shocked by my relationship with Hop; she had been seeing her own shrink for seven years, had shaken his hand when they first met and had had no physical contact with him since, the mere idea of crying on his shoulder impossible to conceive. Privately, I had long thought that Sophie could do with loosening up a bit and perhaps a few sessions with someone like Hop could be just what the doctor ordered.

One evening she came for her lesson and I opened the door to discover a distraught, highly distressed, pale and trembling shadow of her former self looking at me with tear-filled eyes. 'Sophie,' I cried, 'darling, whatever's the matter?' I somehow got her into the sitting room, settled her on the couch and fed her some restorative brandy. She finally calmed down and I said, 'Do you feel able now to tell me what's upset you so much?'

She nodded her head, looked at me, took a deep breath and said in a faltering voice, 'Last week when we were discussing our psychiatrists, you mentioned yours by name, and your cuddly Jungian and my austere Freudian... *are one and the same!*' We looked at each other for several seconds until I shrieked with laughter and fell on the floor clutching my sides as tears of mirth streamed down my face.

'You have *got* to be kidding,' I said as soon as speech became possible, 'tell me you didn't mean that. It simply isn't feasible.' But she did and it was! I rushed off to see Hop the very next day and asked him how such a situation could ever have arisen.

'Well,' said Hop, 'when Sophie first came to see me, she said, "I want an orthodox Freudian analysis." "Fine," I said, "lie down on the couch."'

'But how could I think I was having Jungian and she Freudian?' I demanded to know. He then told me that he had

had a Freudian training but a Jungian analysis, and as a result his approach was eclectic. He chuckled quietly to himself.

'Oh dear,' he said, 'does Sophie think I'm having an identity crisis?'

So... my point is: the guy was good. And for months I'd been telling Hop about this uptight, repressed lady who was obviously wasting her time with her Freudian and needed a few sessions with *him*, and Sophie had been telling him about this highly emotional actress who hurled herself at her shrink whenever the mood took her, and surely this sort of behaviour was well outside the bounds of propriety and perhaps this doctor should be struck off? I never saw Sophie again after that – I realised that I didn't in fact want to be a psychodrama therapist – and hope to this day that she recovered from her massive shock and learned to cuddle Hop very soon after.

What was extraordinary about my relationship with Hop was his ability to make me feel secure within it: to provide a place of safety where I felt able to express the depth of my need to belong, to be a part of; and yet never venture beyond the boundaries that were essential to the discipline of psychotherapy. How he achieved this I am at a loss to describe – it was a great art; but I feel intuitively that the merging of his formidable intelligence, constant compassion and complete lack of ego were key factors in his chameleon abilities. I once said to him, 'Hop, do you fancy me?' He paused, thoughtfully considering the question. The lengthening silence was finally broken when he said, 'There's no easy answer to that...' I laughed at the cleverness of his answer until I could laugh no more, and have dined out on the story ever since.

Shortly after taking up residence in my now legitimately acquired home I began rehearsals for a new play called *Otherwise Engaged*. It was written by Simon Gray, starred Alan Bates and was being directed by Harold Pinter. We were to open at the Oxford Playhouse and a month later transfer to the West End and take up occupancy in the Queen's Theatre on Shaftesbury Avenue. Such excitement! I had long been under the spell of the astonishingly beautiful Alan Bates along with the rest of the population. He had true star quality; he didn't attract one sex and alienate the other – his appeal was universal and he was at the peak of his fame during this period.

Rehearsals took place in a rather charming church hall in Chelsea and commenced on a sunny spring day in May of 1975. I arrived at the location and met my fellow cast members: Ian Charleson and Nigel Hawthorne, Mary Miller, Julian Glover and Benjamin Whitrow and finally the beautiful Bates. He came over to introduce himself and welcome me to the company. I looked into blue-green eyes, a chiselled face framed by long, lustrous black hair, and a mouth that was full and seriously sensual, and that was it for me really. My cup ranneth over and I carried a torch for him until we finally got together almost twenty years later. With disastrous results…

The play proved to be a huge hit and it was great fun being in the hottest show in town. The drama that took place on stage was equalled by that taking place off it. Harold, who was married to the actress Vivien Merchant, had begun a relationship with Lady Antonia Fraser who was married to Sir Hugh Fraser and mother to their six children. Despite conducting their liaison with great discretion, the press found out and overnight the pavements outside the theatre were filled with paparazzi. Vivien published an interview in one of the less-upmarket newspapers which wasn't really in her best interests, and the tabloids feasted on the fallout of two broken marriages and the pain and heartache of all those involved with the savagery of rabid dogs. I loathe this constant catering to the lowest common denominator, and what it reveals about ourselves, as we continue to collude with those who cater to it by lining their pockets with the lucrative rewards of their 'profession'. Having said that, I was first in the queue for the *Mail* and the *Mirror* when Charles and Di were going through their break-up. Yes, I know: people who live in glass houses…

Harold and Antonia disappeared to a secluded cottage secreted somewhere in the heart of the English countryside – location unknown – and our author Simon Gray stepped into the breach and took the final rehearsal, before the dress rehearsal and opening night the following day. We opened on the hottest night of the year. Sweat poured from the faces of both actors and audience, but despite the discomfort experienced by all we received glowing notices and went on to play to packed houses every night of the run. Alan stayed with us for six months and then left to be replaced by Michael Gambon, a lovely man and brilliant actor. My salary of a hundred pounds per week enabled me to furnish my flat and, when I left the show a year after we opened, my home was complete as was the pleasure I took in it.

I enjoyed my time in *Otherwise Engaged*, and became close not only to Alan, but to Ian Charleson and Nigel Hawthorne as well. Ian was so talented: he had a beautiful singing voice, a great stage presence and a sunny personality. His dressing room was next to mine and we exchanged many confidences and had many laughs as the play progressed. We were the youngest members of the company; our dressing rooms were situated at the top of the building and were so far from the stage that we needed passports and a visa to reach it. I was also becoming more unhinged with each day that passed, a fact that Ian was very aware of and did his best to help me deal with. Many years later I was sitting in a waiting room waiting to see my doctor when my eye caught sight of a notice on the wall. It was advertising the Ian Charleson Wing in the local hospital which cared for patients suffering from HIV/AIDS, and my heart contracted with grief for the loss of this rare and talented boy, to the devastation of this cruel illness which was claiming the lives of so many young and gifted homosexuals.

Although I did some more good work with good directors, playing Nancy in *Eustace and Hilda* and Marianna in *Measure for Measure*, both directed by Desmond Davies, my reputation for being 'barking' preceded me and soon the offers dried up and I was left to contemplate another uncertain future as I confronted the issues revealed in my sessions with Hop and my anguished attempts to deal with them.

I was later asked to play Mary Miller's part in a production of *Otherwise Engaged* at the English Speaking Theatre in Vienna. Unfortunately the actor playing Alan's role – the 'otherwise engaged' character of the title – decided to play the part as someone deeply involved with the lives of the other characters, thus making complete nonsense of the play and rendering it incomprehensible to the audience. That pissed me off somewhat... But I loved Vienna; she seemed to me to be like a woman at the peak of her beauty: opulent, romantic, and totally seductive. I rarely joined the outings that were arranged for visiting companies, preferring the solitude and safety of my rooms at a local boarding house, which further reinforced my reputation for eccentricity.

One day I was called to the telephone in the box office. It was my agent asking me if I would be interested in playing a leading role in a new series for the BBC. It was only for one episode, there wasn't time to get a script to me, but it started rehearsals the day after I returned from Vienna. Never before having experienced the luxury of finishing one job and beginning another immediately after its completion, I accepted with alacrity and so set in motion my four-year involvement with a show called *Blake's 7*.

8
Blake's 7

But before I come to *Blake's 7* I have to introduce a friend I made during the period after I left the London production of *Otherwise Engaged* and prior to the Vienna production.

I was in the hall of my flat one morning collecting my mail and, as I turned to the front door, it opened revealing a young man of about my own age – he turned out to be three years younger – with a long, lithe body, and the too-short trousers favoured (mistakenly in my view) by our American cousins. He had great charm, good looks, grace and warmth. We said 'hello' and he told me that he was an actor/dancer/singer appearing in the Broadway production of *A Chorus Line*, the musical that had recently transferred to London and was playing to packed houses at the Theatre Royal, Drury Lane. He had a six-month contract and had rented the flat on the first floor for the duration. We had 'clicked' immediately, each reflecting something of the other; drawn to each other on a deep, subconscious level, that exploded into our consciousness some years later.

Jim, as I called him (his real as opposed to his stage name), described himself as a 'farm boy from Byhalia, Mississippi', a tiny hamlet on the Memphis/Mississippi border. I went there several times over the following years and found it very beautiful but my enthusiasm was somewhat tarnished by my terror of snakes which resulted in a complete inability to relax completely. But I'm jumping ahead of myself.

Jim and I fell in love with each other, which is not quite as euphoric as it appears. Jim was gay, so the chances of us walking down the aisle and living happily ever after were slim to say the least. However, rose-tinted spectacles firmly in place, I refused to acknowledge reality and loved him with an all-consuming passion. Our relationship was not physical at this time; Jim continued to have lovers, most of whom I met, and I didn't mind at all that the physical side of love was not a factor in our relationship. Because of my sexual history I was rather relieved, but deluded myself that Jim was 'the one'. It never occurred to me that his homosexuality provided me with an 'out' as far as my own sexuality was concerned. Because I was seeing Hop frequently at this time, I provided Jim with psychological insights which I had no right to do, and he had no desire to listen to. 'I'll get there,' he would yell at me, 'but in my own time and my own way.' It was quite a volatile relationship needless to say but always an interesting one.

Jim was the perfect hook on which to project my image of the archetype of the Prince. He was tall, glamorous, romantic and a dancer! He wore clothes well, was always beautifully groomed and smelled delicious. Yes, I do realise that these qualities that so appealed to me were the responses of my ego and reveal me for the shallow, frivolous creature that I am and I make no apology for it which is even worse.

During the six months that Jim lived in the house we saw a great deal of each other and I saw a great deal of *A Chorus Line*! I loved the show – the music, the dancing, the set and the staging. But I hated how it had come about: out-of-work dancers having to spill the beans about their most private lives at the auditions, bleed for the director and then discover that they didn't get the part but their story had been used by the director for the actor who did get it. I found it cheap and exploitative, but it didn't alter the fact that there was a lot of talent on that stage.

When the time came for Jim to leave the show and return to New York where he now lived, both our hearts were heavy; but we promised to write and meet again as soon as the possibility presented itself.

I joined the cast of *Blake's 7* for the sixth episode out of a scheduled thirteen. I was to play Servalan, Supreme Commander of the Terran Federation, the enemy of Blake and his seven, and was contracted for the one episode. When I saw the costume design for my character I was less than impressed; jackboots, a safari suit and a helmet seemed a trifle obvious, and as I had arrived at the first rehearsal with very short hair and had been asked by the producer to retain it for the show, I looked at the designs and thought, 'Teamed with this haircut they might as well cast a man.' So I suggested we go completely in the opposite direction: make her incredibly feminine which would be the opposite of her character and would create a tension which would make her dangerous. Fortunately the idea was accepted and so began a parade of some of the most outrageous costumes I have ever worn, before or since. Some of them worked, some of them were risible and all of them were memorable...

We were filming at Elstree Studios, I think it was, when the producer came to see me in my dressing room. He told me that he was very pleased with the way Servalan was developing and asked me if I would consider working on a few more episodes? Regular work; I nearly bit his hand off. The 'few more episodes' turned into a total of twenty-nine during the four series of thirteen episodes each. I'd been seeing Hop regularly after Jim's departure and we'd been exploring the archetypes in some depth; I was also a tad fragile emotionally, oscillating between overconfident highs and lows of black despair. It was from this rather dodgy psyche that Servalan presented herself and provided me with the roller-coaster ride of my life to date.

For the first two series she was dressed in white; the frocks were a little OTT but nothing too outrageous, and the make-up attractive and reasonably discreet, the nails of serviceable length and unvarnished. Actually, I take that back about none of the frocks being too outrageous: I remember a white leather suit – jacket and full length skirt – with skirt split to the crotch under which were silver tights of an unfortunate thickness which felt, and no doubt looked, like those silver pot scourers, and feet encased in boots decorated with silver braid and tied with bows. The braid edged its way all around the suit including the large collar which I wore up, and on my head was a wide-brimmed Spanish hat. What really worried me was that I made it work... But in series three she evolves into another animal: the frocks become black, the make-up more vivid, the nails long and red and her sexuality overt. Why? What caused that emphatic shift? Aaah! Therein hangs a tale...

When the second series ended I accepted Jim's invitation to visit him in the States. He was appearing in a show in Boston and I was to join him there and perhaps also spend some time visiting his family in Byhalia. I was so excited at the prospect of seeing him again and could hardly contain myself as I walked through into the arrivals area wearing a red-and-white polka-dot dress, red high heels and a red hat covering a very bad haircut. I watched him walk towards me and from his smile I knew he was as happy to see me as I was to see him. We fell into each other's arms laughing with delight, and holding hands we left the airport and took a cab to his apartment. His gig in Boston was for three months, so he'd rented the apartment which meant we had both space and privacy.

I went to see the show that evening. It was cabaret performed by one black and one white couple; they were all excellent and I enjoyed myself enormously. Jim had two solos, one of which was *A Nightingale Sang in Berkeley Square*, which he sang beautifully and was to haunt me for many years to come. Then he took me to dinner and that night in Boston, at the age of thirty-five, I ceased to be a teetotaller and discovered the delights of champagne and good wine. I took to both like the proverbial duck to water and haven't looked back since. Back at his apartment he also introduced me to the 'weed'. I'd had a couple of puffs around the age of twenty-three but that was it; so to be introduced to some very good grass after my earlier encounter with champagne, and being a virgin in both those areas, it didn't require many puffs before I was in another dimension of reality altogether and convinced I was a fairy. Jim returned from a bathroom visit and found me perched outside on the window ledge preparing to spread my fairy wings and fly to the nearest fluffy cloud. He hauled me back inside and was rather cross and gave me a lecture on grass and grown-up behaviour. And then we went to bed and made the most wonderful love.

It wasn't erotic, it was beautiful: gentle and tender and full of wonder and completely natural. We felt love and made love and knew love, which for a thirty-two-year-old gay man and a thirty-five-year-old frigid female was a mind-blowing experience, to use the vernacular of the time. I didn't orgasm but it didn't matter; all I wanted was to love him. But after about ten minutes, it all started to go wrong. I am of course exaggerating, but only a little. I was euphoric; we both were initially, but Jim soon saw the impossibility of the situation, which I refused to accept. He knew that despite what had happened between us he was gay and would always want to have relationships with men. I insisted that I had no objection to that, which I didn't at all; I never felt threatened by his homosexuality nor did I view it as a challenge. I accepted him completely as he was, I understood that a man could give him something I never could, but equally I could give him something a man never could. I could never accept another woman in his life, but to be the only woman in his life would be fine by me. Jim could never accept this; his situation was also complicated by the fact that he'd been in a relationship for the past seven years and his and my relationship would be unacceptable to his partner.

Ten days later I left for Byhalia, the growing tension between us striking terror in my heart and causing my behaviour to become increasingly deranged and my sanity questionable.

Jim's mother Helen, a woman of great beauty whom I came to love deeply, introduced me to her friend LaNelle who was the wife of the local preacher, who in turn introduced me to life in a small hamlet in the Deep South of America. One morning we went to a Tupperware meeting held in a church hall. Being at a Tupperware party anywhere was a first for me, but when the ladies started singing, 'We're the Tupperware ladies, we're the best in town,' I felt as though I'd landed on some alien planet which made those in *Blake's 7* look fairly pedestrian by comparison. And try as I might I was unable to share their enthusiasm for the goods on display, and confess I left empty-handed despite a daunting sales pitch from our hostess. I don't think Ann Summers had hit Mississippi at that period and, if it had, can only imagine the reaction of the Tupperware ladies...

Jim's parents, Helen and James Sr, and his younger brother Kenny lived in a small white house deep in the countryside. I found James Sr's habit of chewing tobacco and spitting the resulting juice into the garbage pail rather disconcerting, but their hospitality was wonderful and I was made to feel very welcome. I attended church with them on Sunday mornings and was introduced to the cream of Byhalian society. I visited the home of one lady which was everything I imagined a Southern residence to be – a large house supported by pillars surrounded by a wide wooden balcony with polished mahogany floors – and served mint juleps and iced tea by a maid wearing a black dress and pristine white apron with a white headdress similar to those worn by waitresses in the Lyons teashops in England. I found it all rather surreal and downed more mint juleps than good manners required.

During my stay in Byhalia I had maintained contact with Jim via telephone; our conversations had been brief and unsatisfactory but still unable to dent my euphoria or make me face the inevitable demise of our relationship as lovers. When I eventually returned to Boston, we approached each other warily and it was a visit to Martha's Vineyard that saw us once again become lovers. But with each experience of intimacy our estrangement grew more pronounced. Until... on my last night in Boston we made love for the third and last time. And IT finally happened.

To this day I remain undecided as to what was responsible for this huge milestone in my life. Was it Jim, me, us or the substance he waved under my nose and which I inhaled with dramatic results? It was amyl nitrite, apparently used frequently in the gay community but unheard of by myself. Whatever the cause, it certainly did the trick, and after much reflection I decided that the cause was really irrelevant. A key had been turned, a door opened and I knew a moment of such beauty; a moment I have never been able to repeat. I said to Jim, 'I'm coming,' and I fell through a night sky filled with stars, my soul surrendered itself completely to his and we were indeed in those moments one being, one flesh, united by love.

The next day he took me to Boston airport to catch my flight. As we stood at the barrier he took me in his arms and said, 'I love you more than anything in the world.'

'Then let me stay!' I cried. 'You love me, I love you, we belong together, why are you letting me go?' But let me go he did, and I boarded the aircraft with tears streaming down my face, unable to accept the separation from this man who had revealed to me the beauty of love, the joy of unity and the blessed feeling of home and safety I had experienced in the shelter of his love.

And that is why Servalan appeared in series three with an awareness of her own sexuality, a heightened confidence and sense of herself. But underneath the confident surface was a febrile, manic terror that would erupt with devastating consequences as emotions that I was unable to cope with fought their way inexorably to the surface of my consciousness. What my relationship with Jim had done of course was replicate the abandonment by my mother; it was inevitable that this would happen, and I would continue to repeat that pattern of unsuitable love object until I had finally resolved and accepted the initial loss of my mother.

During my time on *Blake's 7* I became close to the writer Tanith Lee, who wrote the episode *Sand* for me which appeared in series four. We saw a lot of each other and established a ritual of meeting for dinner quite frequently at the Café Royal. Tanith was very beautiful with sea-green eyes, long blonde hair, flawless skin and a stunning figure. We both favoured period frocks and would always arrive for our dinner looking as though we had just stepped off the set of a 1930s movie. We took it in turns to pay and on this occasion it fell to me to foot the bill. As I was seriously without funds I could only hope that my overloaded credit card could rise to the occasion. The Café Royal was many things, but cheap wasn't one of them...

We enjoyed an excellent meal, lots of bubbles and some fine wine. At a table opposite sat a group composed of a white couple and an Arab gentleman, whose eye caught mine several times during the course of the evening. His friends left, but he remained seated at the table. I thought no more about it and, my trepidation somewhat soothed by alcohol, I asked the waiter to bring our bill. He left the table only to return moments later to tell me that the gentleman seated opposite had already paid it and would be delighted if we would join him for coffee. What a gent! Join him we did and he proved himself to be a delightful companion.

He left with Tanith's telephone number and that was the last I expected to see of him. His name was Hussein; he was from Saudi Arabia and intended to return there shortly. So imagine my surpise when I answered my telephone the next day to find him on the line inviting me to join him for dinner at the Dorchester Hotel where he was staying. Apparently he had called Tanith and it was she who furnished him with my number. Having been convinced that it was Tanith who had attracted his attention, I was delighted to find that it was I he wished to pursue. I'd never been good at spotting when a man was interested in me. If he ripped off my clothes, pinned me against a wall and presented me with an erect member, the thought that would go through my mind was: 'Play your cards right Jack, and you could be in with a chance here girl.' But as nothing of the kind had occurred with Hussein I'd assumed his interest was for Tanith.

So I joined him for dinner at the Dorchester every night for the remainder of his stay and I think it's safe to say that the *affaire* that resulted from these meetings was one enjoyed by us both. I mention this now because Hussein was to re-enter my life some years later at a time when I was at my most lost and vulnerable, and his care and kindness threw a light onto the darkness that had become my world.

It was after series three that my financial situation became rather pressing. Unable to accept Jim's rejection, I flew to New York several times to try to convince him to change his mind. I also phoned him frequently, and transatlantic flights and telephone calls made serious inroads into my bank balance. One night he arrived home from one of the gay clubs that proliferated in New York in the late seventies and early eighties to find me sitting on his doorstep. He was far from thrilled to see me but took me upstairs to his flat. I begged him to make love to me again – my pride having long since flown out of the window. After much pleading on my part and with great reluctance on his, victory was mine. But it was a pyrrhic victory; our coupling proving to be less than ecstatic, the joy of our previous encounter long gone and my desolation and panic total. Far from being able to accept the situation, my obsession for Jim – for such it was – increased and my inability to accept the demise of our affair increased with it.

After my overdraft reached £5,000 and my bank manager was having to answer uncomfortable questions from head office as to why he had agreed to advance this amount to a customer who had no collateral to offer and only uncertainty as to future employment prospects, I found I had to make a difficult decision. My flat was in a very expensive area of London and worth a small fortune on the open market. Naturally my landlords were anxious to get rid of a rent-controlled tenant who under the terms of the law at that time had lifelong security of tenure and could pass it on twice to members of her family. If I remained in the flat there would be very little advantage to themselves, so they felt it more than worth their while to offer me £16,000 for vacant possession. I did *not* want to leave my home, but I could see no way of being able to pay back the bank without the injection of cash offered by my landlords. And so finally I accepted their offer and, after seven years and taking only two suitcases of clothes with me, I left my home and everything it contained and headed off to my future in a rented room in the home of a friend in Herne Hill.

My friend was the milliner Shirley Davies, whom I had worked with on *Blake's 7*: a wonderful woman with a huge heart and great warmth who did everything she could to make me feel welcome and comfortable. She shared her home with her two teenaged children, Kevin and Keeley, Eddie her on-off lover, an Irish wolfhound called Finnigan and an endless assortment of cats who left deposits all over the house, particularly the bathroom, many of which I skidded on as I groped my way to the facilities every morning. The house was always full of friends, wine was consumed in copious amounts and Shirl cooked vast dinners in industrial-sized saucepans for all and sundry. After my ordered and solitary life of the previous seven years it appeared chaotic and confused, but it wasn't at all; just very lived-in and extremely free.

I met Malcolm at Shirl's, a gay friend who was looking for somewhere to live, so after some discussion we agreed to look for a house together. We found somewhere quite soon, in somewhere very unlikely like Ruislip; but soon after that Mal saw an advert for a houseboat on the Thames at Chelsea

Reach. He'd lived on a houseboat before and loved it, so we went to see the owner, secured the deal and shortly afterwards we moved into MTB 219 as she was called.

Life on the river totally suited my romantic nature; the ducks bobbing past the portholes, the ebb and flow of the tide, the light from the Hovis building opposite casting its blue glow on the water as night rose to claim the day. When the tide came in and the boat lifted off the mud flats onto which it had settled and rose gently as the water gathered her in its embrace, the motion as we rocked back and forth replicated that of the womb and soothed and calmed those it housed. MTB had fought in the Second World War, as the imprint of a shell in one of the cabins confirmed, and in the quiet of night I imagined I could hear the shouts of the men who had manned her during those turbulent years.

Unfortunately Malcolm turned out to be a bad lot with designs on the remainder of my nest egg, it being reduced from £16,000 to £8,000 after settling my debt with the Nat West and paying off sundry outstanding bills. One morning he took me to a rather smart shop in Queensway and in the sale bought me a mink coat on the never-never. Not being as conscious then as I am today of the horrors that factory-farmed mink have to undergo I was absolutely thrilled with my gift and lost no opportunity to wear it. But Malcolm's desire to continue living with me was replaced by his desire to live with his latest lover; and, recognising that getting control of my assets was proving to be unachievable, left the boat and me to our own devices. However, he demanded the return of the coat so he could sell it and get some of his money back. I refused to return it; he had reneged on our deal to remain on the boat for a year and was leaving me with all the financial responsibility, which was patently unfair.

And so he began his campaign to acquire it by more devious means. I would leave the boat in order to attend rehearsals, making sure that the door and portholes were securely locked, only to find on my return that he had somehow managed to gain entry. My possessions would be rearranged, objects moved and the terror I felt at his sinister attempts to drive me out of what remained of my mind was acute. But I still refused to return *the coat*; a principle was at stake. This man had offered me friendship and protection; he was well aware of how mentally fragile I was and did everything he could to push me over the edge to which I was so perilously close. My refusal to concede to his demands eventually wore him down; I retained the coat, and he ceased his attempts to drive me to madness. But his campaign to terrorise me had taken its toll, and my behaviour became increasingly erratic and unpredictable.

I was beyond lost, my sense of self non-existent and my behaviour completely out of character. I had long since had a reputation for being outrageous and OTT but had always managed to remain just within the bounds of accepted decency. No longer. I would walk the streets in full evening dress, tears streaming down my face, desperate to find some relief from the pain that overwhelmed me. One night I raised my dress and urinated in the gutter. The entire procedure was witnessed by a party dining in the window of the restaurant opposite me; I saw the appalled expressions on their faces as they watched this seemingly respectable woman reduced to the level of something primitive and alien. I felt such deep, deep shame as I stumbled off into the darkness, as well as confusion and bewilderment at the depths to which I had so obviously sunk. How had I allowed myself to become so reduced; how could I shine a light into the darkness of the world I now inhabited, how could I escape the unbearable pain that was my constant companion? I had no answers to these questions.

The title of this chapter is *Blake's 7* but my references to it are slight, and I'm sure very unsatisfactory to those readers who wish to hear about the show in great depth and detail. Because my memories of the series are dominated by the trauma of my emotional state at the time, because I was more mad than sane, I have no fund of witty and amusing stories to relate; no revealing anecdotes to tell about my fellow cast members, no desire to respond to questions about how it felt to walk through quarries in full evening dress and four-inch heels. Those questions seem trivial and of little consequence as I view from a distance of thirty years the desolation that engulfed me during that almost unendurable period of my life. I apologise to those I have disappointed and can only hope that in attempting to write the truth of my state of mind I will be forgiven, and perhaps gain some understanding from those who forgive me of my profound despair.

I will alway be grateful to *Blake's 7* for providing me with the opportunity to create a character: to play someone for the first time. She made quite an impact and has since become an icon; but more than being simply a part I played, she was a powerful force in my private life demanding that I recognise aspects of my character of which I had previously had no inkling. One night as I sat alone on MTB I became aware of a separation taking place in my head. I was aware that something had split off and detached itself from 'reality'. For a few brief moments I experienced a detachment that was devoid of any human emotion and for those brief moments I occupied the mind of the psychopath; I had no compassion or empathy for the emotions of others, only a ruthless lust for the domination provided by power and control. It was a mercifully brief but terrifying experience and has never been repeated, but it gave me an insight into and an understanding of the deranged mind of the criminally insane. I understand that psychopaths are the result of nature not nurture. They are born that way and no cure is possible, which is a pretty bleak prognosis. I was lucky; I observed the mindset but remained ultimately uncontaminated by it.

TOP LEFT Me aged two   TOP RIGHT Me aged four
BOTTOM Me and Rosamund Ward at the dreaded Marist Convent

TOP LEFT & RIGHT Early portrait shots
BOTTOM Rehearsing Anouilh's *Restless Heart* with Amanda Murray at RADA, 1963

Publicity still for *Don't Raise the Bridge, Lower the River*, 1966

In my flat on the Old Brompton Road around 1979

TOP LEFT That seventies look... TOP RIGHT In profile (Photo © Joel O'Sullivan)
BOTTOM Susan Fleetwood and me in *White Mischief*

TOP *White Mischief* – me in the front row, John Hurt at the back holding his hat
BOTTOM In *Night and Day* at the Belgrade Theatre, Coventry with John Bowles

As Servalan in *Blake's 7*
Photo © Moviestore Collection/Rex Features

A glamour shot by Joel
Photo © Joel O'Sullivan

9
Aftermath

I returned to the BBC to record the fourth and final series of *Blake's 7*, but the momentum had gone; the scripts appeared for the most part repetitive and lacking in imagination, something felt not only by the cast but also the viewers as I discovered after it had been aired. I was permanently exhausted, physically, mentally and emotionally. My state of mind was patently obvious to my fellow cast members who showed me great kindness at this time, but it was apparent that a complete breakdown was on the cards.

I was prey to every kind of conman and opportunist, one of whom remains vividly in my mind. I met him socially and thereafter he would frequently visit me. He would play soft music that would lull me into a completely false sense of security. One evening he dressed himself in a white sheet; he wound it around his body several times, the final effect being of a long robe worn in biblical times. He asked me for a knife and I went into the kitchen to find one. I had no idea what he wished to do with it; the fact that he might have intended to kill me with it crossed my mind but I greeted the idea with complete equanimity and even a sense of joy. I gave him the knife and he plunged it into his breast; unfortunately it wasn't as sharp as he would have wished and in order to draw blood required a second attempt. This proved successful as blood trickled down his chest. So fascinated was I by this procedure that I was unable to hear the words he kept repeating. They finally penetrated into my madness, and I was aware that he was repeating, 'Drink my blood, drink my blood.'

And so I did. I think I should make clear that the blood wasn't gushing out, so it proved unnecessary to drink it; it was more of a lapping than a gulping. He then commanded me to look at his forehead; as I did so, I watched stigmata appear there. They remained for quite some moments before fading and finally disappearing. 'Now you belong to me,' he said.

Fortunately this prophecy proved false and I have remained my own woman. He definitely possessed some powers, but I suggest they could have been put to better use than his attempts to hypnotise a deranged and seriously disturbed woman who wanted only to 'belong' to someone and was seemingly prepared to go to any lengths to achieve her aim and thus obliterate the isolation that engulfed her.

After finishing *Blakes* I spent eighteen months 'resting', becoming increasingly difficult to live with as I endured the angst experienced by every unemployed actor and which never seems to become any easier. So imagine my joy when a large package with 'BBC' stamped upon its front thudded through the letterbox one particularly desolate morning (the desolation being my state of mind that is, not the weather). I ripped it open, tearing cuticles on the staples inside, and triumphantly held aloft three slightly bloodstained scripts and a letter from the director.

The scripts turned out to be three episodes of *Doctor Who* entitled *The Two Doctors*, to be filmed on location in Spain with the two doctors of the title being Patrick Troughton and Colin Baker. As I believe I've already made clear I'm not a sci fi fan and have to confess to never having seen *Doctor Who* in my life! And although to be completely honest I would have preferred my first job after *Blakes* not to have been another sci fi in outer space but a romantic comedy set in Rome, I was delighted – to put it very mildly – to have the opportunity of working with Colin Baker. I had first seen him in a series called *The Brothers* back in the seventies, and along with the vast majority of the female sex had fallen totally in lust with him. He was sex on legs. The character he was playing was the 'baddie' and Colin made him irresistibly attractive. My girlfriend Mo and I used to have long chats after each episode about just how devastatingly attractive we found him because he *was* so bad, and why women found 'baddies' so much more interesting than 'goodies' etc; and now I was being invited to work with him! What shone through in his work, and was the main reason – Mo and I decided – for his sexiness, was his intelligence. That boy knew what he was doing and I was fascinated by the mind that produced that performance.

I was being offered a part in the three episodes by the director Peter Moffatt with whom I had worked many years before. I immediately accepted and reported to the BBC for a wig and costume fitting. It turned out that another actress had been hired initially for the part but had had to drop out due to illness, and I inherited not only her part but her wig and costume as well. Time was very short and there was no option other than for me to go with the wig and costume that had been designed for the original actress. Unfortunately the wig made me look like a very poor man's Elizabeth Taylor playing Widow Twankey, and the costume did very little, if indeed anything at all, for me. Altogether not my best look. When my wig was lost in transit to Spain, which meant I was able to spend three days by the pool with Pat Troughton while frantic attempts were made to locate it (all unsuccessful), and eventually had to visit a barber in Seville – I kid you not – to have a wig made for me, I couldn't have been more thrilled.

I boarded the coach that was to take us to the airport to catch our flight to Seville and was immediately caught up in the heady, holiday atmosphere that hit me as soon as I stepped on board. I love being on location and able to devote myself totally to the job in hand; no schlepping home after work to the gas bill, the laundry and all the mundane tasks which have to be fulfilled in order to enable the wheels of domesticity to run smoothly. On location everything is taken care of and actors are treated like the children they really are: told when to get up, dressed by their dresser and made-up by their make-up artist, brought breakfast by the third assistant, popped into a car and taken to the location, told what to say and how to say it, fed and watered; and at the end of the day they are popped back into the car and returned to the hotel, undressed by their dresser, have their make-up removed by their make-up artist, and dinner brought to them on a tray via room service. They then go out to play and meet each other by the pool – in this instance – drink a great deal, laugh even more and generally behave appallingly until the most grown-up among their number mumbles that bed might be a good idea as we have about three hours left before we're on call again.

I loved every second of my time on *Doctor Who* and laughed until I cried at the wit supplied by my hero and his sidekick Frazer Hines. When we were in the studio I was shooting a scene with Laurence Payne and Frazer was standing behind me. I was playing an Androgum (don't ask) and was asking Laurence, who had apparently created me, if he could make another one as I would like a companion. My line was: 'I would like you to make me a consort.' When I heard Frazer say, 'I don't think we've got enough milk,' I fell to my knees and cried with laughter.

I sat next to my hero on the plane and very soon found myself calling him Col; being advised to give up the weed – to no avail I might add – and revelling in the sharpness of his mind, his quick wit and intrinsic kindness. By the time we reached our destination we knew we adored each other and continue to do so to this day. Some years later I was invited to a *Doctor Who* convention in Chicago and discovered to my joy that Col was also on the guest list. We met up and after a rapturous reunion he said, 'I've suggested you for Amanda in a production of *Private Lives*, you're born to play her darling. Get in touch with your agent as soon as you get back to

London.' I did, went to meet the director and was offered the part. A three-month tour of the Middle and Far East playing Amanda in *Private Lives*; I was ecstatic. I immediately sent Col a huge bouquet thanking him for his help and signed the card, 'Amanda'. I was somewhat disconcerted not to hear from him and when next we met asked him if he had received the flowers.

'What flowers?' he queried.

'The ones I sent you after I got the job you put me up for. I signed the card "Amanda".'

'It was *you*,' he said as comprehension dawned. 'I couldn't think who the hell had sent them; I don't know anybody called Amanda and I had quite a lot of explaining to do to Marion. Of course; it was *you!*' We laughed quite a lot over that faux pas.

As already mentioned, thanks to my missing wig I had three days off while it was sorted and, as Pat Troughton was also free, we spent our time lazing by the pool, drinking cocktails and chatting. I had worked with Pat's son David in a BBC production of *David Copperfield* and had fond memories of filming with him at Great Yarmouth, I think it was, and being aware that he was a talented boy destined I felt to do well in the business, which he certainly has. Pat and I discussed everything under the sun: philosophy, religion, spirituality, life after death and reincarnation, until our intellectual musings were shattered as the rest of the company returned from filming and divebombed into the pool. I was fortunate to spend that time with Pat; he was a good man and true and very much loved within the company.

I finally saw the barber in Seville, who managed to cobble together an acceptable wig, and was then able to begin filming. We were on location somewhere in Andalucia and what remains indelibly printed in my mind is the heat. The temperature was in the nineties and as I emerged from the make-up trailer into the searing heat of the sun it took no time at all for my wig to become unglued as my head released large drops of perspiration, which then rolled down my face leaving smudged mascara and wrecked foundation. As swiftly as it was repaired it became ruined again, and I wondered what idiot had decided that filming in heavy costumes – some of which were made of rubber – would be a good idea at the height of a Spanish summer.

Somehow we found the energy to embrace the difficulties of the day and all was well until the final two days. I woke up unable to move my top lip. I rushed to the bathroom mirror and saw that my entire top lip was covered in tiny, very painful blisters. The hotel doctor was summoned who informed me that I was suffering from herpes and could probably expect to get reoccurrences for the rest of my life. He left me with antibiotics and some cream to apply, and our director with the problem of how to photograph an actress with festering pustules on a previously pristine visage. So for the last two days I was either shown in a very, very long shot or with my back to camera. I had never had herpes before and thank God it hasn't reappeared since. Before we started shooting, I had creamed off my moustache and think I made the mistake of going into the sun too soon afterwards. The intense heat of the sun must have reacted badly with the chemicals in the cream. That's the only explanation I can think of, and I've been careful not to make the same mistake since!

When I finally walked away from *Blakes* for the last time I had to make a decision regarding my financial future. I had £8,000 remaining of my money from the flat, and a reputation for being unemployable. So, previous experience notwithstanding, I booked a flight to Los Angeles to try my luck once again in the city of the angels. It was an ill-conceived idea and ended disastrously, as anyone with a brain in their head could have predicted.

I was met in LA by my friend Bob and taken to the Chateau Marmont. I had no plan of how I was going to achieve my ambition of gaining work; I had no contacts to follow up and no idea of how to obtain work in a town notoriously hard to break into. The Chateau Marmont was not cheap, so after a week I moved into an hotel on Sunset Strip. It was a bleak place; the rooms were grimy and redolent with the despair of the many lives that had previously occupied them. My fellow guests were, for the most part, transients: hookers and their pimps, and girls like myself desperate for a 'break'.

Bob would leave me on a Friday evening and return on Monday morning. He always told me not to leave the hotel as I was in a particularly dangerous area and he couldn't guarantee my safety if I strayed from the hotel. One evening I put on my mink coat and such jewellery as I possessed and walked the length of the Strip several times, praying that some drug addict would attack and hopefully kill me. Alas, it never happened. I returned to my room feeling ill; as I knelt on the floor of the bathroom vomiting into the porcelain I raised my head and leant on my arms cradling the lip of the lavatory bowl. As I did so, I watched a large cockroach scuttle past; saw the dirt that encrusted the pedestal, and the stained linoleum I was kneeling on. 'How did this happen to me,' I asked myself; 'how did I get here?' I had no answer to these questions; could see no way of escaping my self-created reality.

During one of the breaks between series of *Blakes* I had worked on a production of *Witness for the Prosecution* directed by a man called Robert Henderson. The story revolves around two people: an older woman, played by myself, and her much younger lover who unfortunately was played by a man who was not only older than I was but very much looked it. Apparently he had made a career out of playing the part for many years and should have given it up decades previously. Needless to say, the production was a disaster and did not appear on my CV. But Robert, who was seventy-three, was the toy-boy husband of the actress Estelle Winwood who was ninety-nine and living in Hollywood. Robert had written to her asking if she would allow me to stay with her while I found my feet, so to speak, in LA. A letter of confirmation arrived at

Bob's house; and, feeling that things were finally looking up, I packed my bags and left for the Valley in Pasadena.

I arrived at the address I had been given and nervously rang the bell. The door was opened by Obelia, Estelle's maid, who greeted me warmly and showed me into the sitting room. 'Miss Winwood will be right with you,' she said as she closed the door and left the room. I was wearing a 1940s black suit and a pillbox hat with a veil. I heard the door slowly open and saw in the doorway a tiny figure, one gnarled hand clutching a walking stick, and wearing a hat (into which a slightly askew wig had been stitched) atop a heavily made-up face. The application of said make-up left a great deal to be desired: one eyebrow distinctly higher than its companion, the foundation orange in colour and ending at her chin and, with red lipstick smeared across thin lips, the entire effect somewhat grotesque and quite alarming. She slowly shuffled into the room and fixed her hostile eyes upon me.

'Who are you, what do you want?' she enquired, her voice surprisingly deep coming from so small a body. I explained who I was and that her husband had written to her asking if I could stay with her and she had graciously consented. She denied all knowledge of having received any communication from her husband and demanded that I leave her house immediately. Fortunately, Obelia entered the room at this juncture (I later learned she had been listening outside the door) and held aloft not only Robert's letter but a copy of the one Estelle had sent to him. 'Then I suppose you'd better stay,' she muttered ungraciously, and I thankfully followed Obelia to the guest suite: a light sunny room decorated in a warm shade of yellow with a bathroom attached to it. I was enchanted with my new home; the scent of magnolias filled the room, the orange trees, heavy with fruit, outside my window filled me with joy and my spirits lifted for the first time in weeks.

Initially I felt great compassion for Estelle; she appeared to be surrounded by a coterie of young gay men who spent her money freely dining in lavish restaurants – although she accompanied them, she rarely ate anything – and wanted to protect her from being exploited. However, my compassion was short-lived as she quickly revealed herself to be a dominating, domineering old witch, impossible to like or help. I was required to push her around in her wheelchair quite frequently and, as our relationship was threatening to degenerate into a real-life version of *Whatever Happened to Baby Jane?* and the urge to release the handbrake and send her hurtling to her demise down the nearest steep hill became more pronounced, I went to Obelia one afternoon after a particularly frustrating session with 'Madam' and exclaimed, 'If someone put a pillow over that old bat's face one night and held it there until she expired, they would be doing a great service to humanity!'

'That woman is too mean to die!' cried Obelia. 'She bin sent to the Actors Home twice, an' twice they sent her back, and they's used to dealing with difficult ol' folks, but even they couldn't cope with that ol' witch!'

One of my duties was to take her nightcap of whiskey and ginger ale to her bedroom last thing at night. I always enjoyed going to her bedroom: it was a time warp from the 1930s – certainly Hollywood's idea of an actress's bedroom of that era. The walls were covered in silk, the curtains a heavy red velvet with deep pelmets, kept permanently drawn, the dressing table covered with enormous scent bottles and the room dominated by the high canopied bed draped in matching red velvet. Despite the outside temperature, which was in the high nineties, the heating was constantly on. On this particular night, I entered the room, placed the glass on her bedside table, wished her goodnight and turned to leave. But before I could do so, a hand shot out of the bed and grasped my wrist, holding it with surprising strength for a ninety-nine-year-old. She was still wearing the hat, the withered body encased in a nightgown covered with stains from the previous night's whiskey. I looked at her with some astonishment as the thin lips drew back to form a grimace which was her parody of a smile and heard her say, 'You can get in with me if you like…'

My sexual history is littered with unappetising advances from inappropriate sources, but never before – or indeed since – had I been propositioned by a ninety-nine-year-old woman. The bizarreness of the situation rendered me temporarily speechless. As her grip on my wrist tightened, I somehow managed to prise her fingers off it, muttered something incomprehensible and fled to the sanctuary of my own quarters. But the nightmare didn't end there.

Early the following morning, a knock on my door caused me to leap from my bed; after my hastily shouted 'come in', it opened to reveal two police officers. We looked at each other and, somewhat confused by their presence (and never having been a 'morning' person), I asked how I could assist them. It transpired that Estelle, in return for my rebuff the previous evening, had telephoned the Pasadena Police Department asking them to eject me from her property. They were extremely apologetic, but as it was indeed Madam's house they had no alternative but to comply with her request. Should I refuse, arrest, handcuffs and a prison cell were my only available options. What could I do? I quickly packed, threw on some clothes, was escorted to the front door where I was hugged by a tearful Obelia, and somewhat stunned found myself outside on the pavement. As I stood there surrounded by suitcases, a friend of Estelle's – the only one she had left and whom I had met once before – drew up in her car. 'What's going on?' she asked me. I explained my predicament and this kind woman immediately cancelled her intended visit to my ejector, told me to get into her car and drove me to her house. She apologised for only being able to offer me a couch in her sitting room and garage space in which to hang my clothes, but told me I was welcome to stay with her until I found alternative accommodation. I was well and truly 'saved by the bell' and will always remember 'the kindness of strangers' as demonstrated by that generous soul.

A matter of days later I received a telephone call from Hussein. He was in San Francisco and had somehow managed to trace me to my present address. He told me that he would be in the States for a few more days and there was a ticket waiting for me at LAX airport if I would like to join him in San Francisco. So I folded up the put-you-up bed, took some clothes from the garage and left for San Fran and the five-star hotel in which Hussein was staying. My life is full of such extremes, not always pleasant; but for this one I was extremely grateful.

I spent three days with Hussein, and his care, compassion and humanity enabled me to gain some much needed strength. One morning as he was leaving for a business meeting, he asked me if I would go into town and find some suitable presents for his three young daughters, all of them under the age of ten. 'I'd love to,' I told him and, taking a fistful of dollars from him, left for one of the smartest shops San Francisco provided. I spent a glorious morning buying the sort of party frocks beloved by young girls and matching them with white tights and silver Mary Jane shoes. When Hussein returned that evening he was delighted with my purchases but completely taken aback when I gave him the change from the fistful of dollars and receipts for my expenditure. He looked at the money and then looked at me.

'The only women I have given money to in the past have been prostitutes, but you are not a prostitute,' he said. 'I fully expected you to keep whatever money remained, you were welcome to it, but you have returned it. I know you are deeply distressed at the moment, and I hope that spending these few days with me has given you some slight comfort. If I can ever be of assistance to you in the future, you have only to call me.' I never did – indeed that was the last contact I ever had with him – but I shall always remember him and wish him nothing but love.

Before I had left England, during a final session with Hop he'd asked me if I had medical insurance for my forthcoming visit to LA. I'd looked at him blankly. 'No,' I said, 'it never occurred to me that I should need it.' He looked at me and said, very gently, that it 'might be an idea'. So off I trotted and arranged some. What wise advice that proved to be! After bidding farewell to Hussein in San Francisco I returned to Pasadena, and a few days later was found wandering the streets in my dressing gown. An ambulance was called and I was taken to the Las Encinas Hospital for the mentally disturbed. The inevitable breakdown had finally arrived.

10
Sanctuary

I spent six weeks in the Las Encinas Hospital for the mentally disturbed, and thanked God on more than one occasion for Hop's suggestion that medical insurance 'might be a good idea': the alternative would have been the county hospital and it's quite possible that if taken there I might have remained for a long, long time! My ability to take care of myself – always dodgy at the best of times – had long deserted me; for months I had been living off adrenaline, very little food, prescription drugs, appalling Californian champagne, cigarettes and not much else. When I finally hit rock bottom and found myself totally dependent upon the ministrations of the staff for my survival, my relief was immense. I could go no further, my will to live was non-existent, my despair overwhelming.

I phoned an old friend from my RADA days, now a major Hollywood star, told him what had happened and where I was and asked if he would come to visit me. He refused. 'Kill yourself,' he said, 'nobody will care. You were always mad, accept that and end it.' At the time his reaction seemed extremely harsh, but with hindsight I can understand it. If someone with dodgy marbles had called me with the same request, I may well have refused to see them – but hopefully with a little more compassion than he showed me.

FROM BYFLEET TO THE BUSH

Initially I was put into a room in the main body of the hospital and shared it with another patient. In the grounds were chalets where one could live alone and after much pleading on my part and reluctance on the doctor's part I was eventually transferred to my own chalet. The hospital grounds were very beautiful: rich with flowers, palm trees, and a spectacular monkey puzzle tree. Nature has always provided me with great solace, and the comfort I took from the beauty of my surroundings afforded me some measure of peace.

For my entire stay I wore a long black lace négligée with matching peignoir and a black pillbox hat with a half veil, and carried a beaded 1930s evening bag. I certainly looked the part as I roamed the grounds passing other patients who were dressed in perhaps more appropriate clothing. I was given drugs to subdue my anxiety and received daily visits from my therapist. I also took part in group therapy sessions and diligently attended occupational therapy classes, but despite my best efforts never mastered basket-weaving or discovered an ability to turn lumps of plasticine into recognisable shapes. I'd always lacked any talent with my hands and was unable to develop any during my hospital stays.

One morning I awoke to find my fellow inmates in a state of great excitement. A film company had arrived to do some filming in the grounds. Quite what the production was I never discovered, but suspect it was an episode of one of the many shows that Hollywood was making for television. I made my way to the outside set, my heart pounding with excitement as I saw a world that was so familiar to me. Barriers had been set up to keep the 'inmates' at an acceptable distance, but I was able to penetrate them and made my way to the edge of the set. Immediately the assistant director appeared, megaphone in hand and flanked by several security guards. I was asked to leave the set immediately and return to the patients' side of the barrier.

'But I'm an actress,' I told him. 'I understand your world because it is also mine, please may I stay and watch you film?'

He looked at my bizarre clothing, took in my frantic manner, and nodded to the security men who assisted me firmly but gently to the hospital side of the barrier. 'Please, please let me stay,' I cried, 'I know how to behave, I won't get in your way or intrude, you won't even know I'm here!'

Tears were streaming down my face but my appeals fell on deaf ears as the security men delivered me into the hands of a male nurse and quickly retreated from this obvious 'nutter'. I was given an injection and put to bed; and that was the extent of my Hollywood film career!

I came to know several of my fellow patients. Some were women who came regularly once or twice a year for a few weeks in order to recover from the stresses of marriage to difficult (but very rich) men; a lot were depressives, some were psychotic but all were obviously disturbed. One man in particular caught my attention; he was always alone and never appeared to speak to anyone. I got into the habit of sitting next to him; we never spoke but there was a tacit understanding between us that we both derived great comfort from each other. One day he spoke to me and I held his hand as he did so. We never said a great deal to each other but we found a peace together that was infinitely precious to us both. I later discovered that he had been in the hospital for many years, and after many attempts to treat his condition had failed – apparently he was very violent – he had been given a lobotomy. Since the operation he had never spoken once, so his verbal communication with me was seen as a great breakthrough. But he never spoke to anyone else; so what had triggered his response to me? I can only conclude that our connection was on a very deep level; we intuited each other's pain and alienation, isolation and grief. Neither of us had ever experienced any sense of 'belonging' in a world we both found terrifying in its incomprehensibility, and we each recognised the 'madness' that had engulfed us as a result. A shared sensitivity was the bridge that connected us. When the time came for me to leave the hospital, I said goodbye to my lobotomised friend with great reluctance. We held each other and I felt the love flow between us and could only hope that that love would sustain us in our separate futures. Wherever you are now, my friend, that love is still alive and active, and I hope so much that it is of some small comfort to you in the pain of isolation.

Soon after arriving at the hospital I became aware that my bottom was itching rather a lot. I mentioned it to one of my nurses and an appointment was made for me to see a proctologist at a neighbouring medical hospital. I duly made the journey in an ambulance accompanied by two male nurses, and on arrival submitted to the examination of the botty specialist.

'Miss Pearce,' he said after completing his examination, 'you have a lesion in your rectum; do you have any idea how this might have occurred?'

'Yes!' I responded brightly, delighted to be of assistance, 'I had this Middle Eastern lover and we indulged in this quaint Middle Eastern practice.'

He then proceeded to lecture me on the appropriate uses of the rectum – rather disapprovingly I felt – and told me I required surgery to solve the problem. In hindsight I feel quite certain that the application of Vaseline would have been a much better remedy for my discomfort than the three hundred and fifty bucks he charged me for the operation. Anyway, a date was arranged for the surgery and, once again accompanied by two male nurses, I returned to the botty doctor to be stitched up (in every sense of the word). I walked into the operating theatre and lay down on the table.

'Not like that,' said Botty Doctor rather testily, and proceeded to turn me over and position me with my back raised in the air, leaning on my elbows and knees.

'Listen sunshine,' I said over my shoulder, 'it was being in this position that got me in this mess in the first place.'

I have no doubt that Botty Doctor was the recipient of many gifts, but alas! a sense of humour was not one of them.

During my stay I was once again obsessed by the need to earn some money – enough to provide me with the secure roof over my head for which I desperately longed. Somewhere I could feel safe, somewhere that wasn't going to be taken from me, somewhere I'd realise the experience of *home*. Needless to say, in the three months I had been in Hollywood I'd managed to rid myself of the eight grand I arrived with and was once again penniless. I'd started to write some (rather bad) poetry and my fevered brain convinced itself that if I could write several volumes of the stuff and sell them, I could maybe make enough dosh to fulfil my need for a home. But, pigs, as they say, might fly. I had to find another way to make the readies I so urgently required; but try as I might, I could find no acceptable answer to my predicament. I could act but had become virtually unemployable and had no other skills or talents to offer that would generate an income to enable me to provide for myself.

I considered selling my body but had no idea how to go about it. Did I have to stand on street corners looking for trade, and if so which corners? I'd once seen a television documentary about 'street walkers' and understood that if you solicited on another hooker's patch you were liable to get a knife in your back, either from the hooker herself or her pimp. Did I need a pimp, and if so, where would I find one? It struck me as being in poor taste to walk up to a likely looking candidate in the street and ask if he would consider pimping for me. Anyway, what did a pimp look like? My only knowledge of this particular breed of gentleman had come from black-and-white films shot in the 1950s where the entire male cast seemed to be composed of East End gangsters all built like brick shithouses with heavily Brylcreemed hair (slicked back and usually black, denoting evil intent) and sharp three-piece suits and carrying guns in artfully concealed shoulder holsters. But I couldn't recall seeing anyone resembling those characters during my numerous forays into Soho to visit Anello & Davide, the shop that supplied the

Royal Ballet Company, in order to purchase the character shoes that comprised my footwear for many years after leaving RADA where I had first been introduced to them. And as I'd never been approached by anyone affecting to be a pimp, offering his services should I require them, I was at a complete loss as to how to go about achieving a life on the streets.

It occurred to me that perhaps there was a magazine or newspaper specifically for 'ladies of the night' where I could advertise for a pimp, wise in the ways of hookerdom, who could guide and advise me in my new career; a sort of weekly news sheet, called something like *Doll's Delight* and containing lots of informative articles by the 'dolls' themselves and carrying advertisements for new 'dolls' requiring the services of a pimp with accompanying telephone numbers to call. But if such a publication *did* exist how could I find out about it and have myself put on its mailing list? I could hardly go up to a girl standing on a street corner in Soho and furtively ask her if she knew where I could purchase the 'hookers' weekly news sheet', only to discover to my chagrin that she was a pearl-necklace-wearing debutante waiting for the lights to change so she could cross the street. I would more than likely find myself arrested, convicted and cast for an indeterminate period of time into prison where I would slip into insanity and be committed to Broadmoor for life.

What else? There must be some way I could support myself. Las Vegas show girl? Couldn't dance or sing so that was out. Croupier? I wasn't absolutely sure what a croupier was; but I thought it was something to do with cards, and as it took me until I was twenty-nine to master 'snap' I knew I would never achieve mastery of the knowledge necessary to preside over card games. I then remembered that a croupier is someone who claws back the chips with a net attached to a pole at the roulette table and nothing at all to do with cards. So: surely I could claw back chips? How much did a croupier earn? Would I get a salary or be dependent on tips; and would either earn me enough to buy a cottage in the country or even a caravan in Cleethorpes? The caravan would be Romany and horse-drawn. (I had always been attracted to the life of the Romany gypsies whenever I'd seen them in the country lanes of England. The brightness of the colours they painted their caravans, the warmth and opulence of the interiors, the richness of the fabrics, the deep mahogany wood and bevelled mirrors enchanted me. I longed to sleep beside the black, pot-bellied, coal-burning stove and watch as it weaved its magic; as flames reflected in the old mirrors softly lit the glowing golds and brilliant blues, ruby reds and poignant pinks of the patchwork velvet quilt that covered me. As I've already mentioned, many years later I learned that my mother was herself a pure-blooded Romany gypsy, making me fifty per cent Romany; so I understood then that my desire for this lifestyle was probably inherited and not simply an unrealistic romantic fantasy.)

I'd be very happy in a horse-drawn wagon; and, as a career as a 'lady of the night' was proving itself to be an extremely remote possibility (and fraught with peril even if achievable) and I had no other skills to offer, if I could just raise the dosh for Dobbin and the wagon, surely I could get by selling pegs or sprigs of heather and reading palms? My chances of finding a practical solution to my financial situation were slim to nil. And anyway, I don't know how to read palms.

Needless to say alcohol was strictly against the rules. However, after I was hospitalised, Bob collected my clothes from my samaritan's garage and brought them to the funny farm for me, and as I unpacked them I came across two boxes of Californian wine, one of each colour, which I had the foresight to conceal from prying eyes. One late afternoon my therapist arrived for our session; by this time we had established a good relationship, and she flung open the door, collapsed into a chair and declared, 'I've just had the day from hell, and right now I would willingly sell my soul for a drink!' My question, 'Red or white?' caused her mouth to gape open as she stared at the bounty I was holding aloft. We both then fell about and spent an hilarious hour feeling like kids behind the bike shed at school as we gleefully broke the no-alcohol rule, got pleasantly plastered and said, 'Yah boo sucks!' to authority.

During my life I've spent quite a lot of time in hospitals – for both mental and physical reasons –and have always found them to be havens of peace and tranquility. In the days when I could afford private health insurance I usually managed to get my money's worth and find myself safely tucked up in a white-sheeted bed awaiting an operation at least once a year. I particularly enjoyed anaesthetics – merciful oblivion – and the sheer relief of handing over responsibility for my wellbeing to those far more competent to deal with it than I, despite my best efforts to get a handle on it. Once when discussing these feelings with Hop he said, 'Hospital is just a form of extended mothering, that's all it is.'

'That'll do', I shot back, quick as a flash, 'bring it on!'

Fortunately, since my efforts to learn to mother myself have vastly improved, so my desire for the protection afforded by the medical profession has greatly diminished. But I will always be grateful for the care and compassion they accorded me during those turbulent years, even if I did have to pay for it. One night during my stay at Las Encinas I was discovered by the night nurse in a highly disturbed state. She called the doctor who examined me and said, 'She needs round the clock nursing.'

'Can she afford it?' questioned the nurse.

I looked at her with horror and said, 'Are you saying that your compassion depends on my ability to pay for it?'

To which the answer was undoubtedly, '*Yes!*'

One day Bob came to visit me and told me that he felt unable to see me any more as he had 'had enough'. Understandable in the circumstances. I was unable to pay him any longer to be my companion, and petrol cost money, so he felt unable to remain in contact. He left and I never saw or heard from him again until some ten years later when I was appearing in *Shadowlands* at the Belgrade Theatre in Coventry. In response to my shout of 'come in' to a knock on my dressing room door after a performance, the door opened and there was Bob. We fell into each other's arms and I listened with great sadness as he told me that he had AIDS and not long left to live.

'You are my only unhealed relationship, sugar,' he said, 'I had to see you.' I was so happy that he had and that we were able to heal the rift between us. We parted as loving friends and he died a few months later. My heart went out to his mother: she had two sons, Bob and his brother Steve, and she lost them both to AIDS.

At the end of six weeks I felt able to leave the hospital and return to London. I was far from well but felt the need to return to Hop and Daryl. Daryl was my body doctor as opposed to my head doctor and one of the kindest and best doctors I have ever known. The first time I visited him for some medical ailment, I was obviously suffering from depression.

'What are you doing about it, dear?' he enquired.

'I'm seeing a psychiatrist,' I told him.

'Jesus Christ Jack,' he said, 'you're depressed, the last thing you need is a psychiatrist! I've never met one who wasn't totally fucked up himself.' Many years later he liaised with Hop via a telephone conversation concerning my good self. He looked at me afterwards and said, 'Sounds like a pretty good bloke, for a psychiatrist.' Praise indeed!

I went to see him once to ask that he remove my coil as I would like to try and become pregnant. A long pause followed this announcement. Finally he said, 'Jesus Christ Jack' (most of our conversations began with Daryl invoking Our Blessed Lord), 'having a baby plays havoc with the hormones and, let's face it, yours are pretty fucking dicey at the best of times, so the thought of taking you through a nine months' pregnancy Jack is awesome.'

So, on this reassuring note, he removed my coil; but despite its removal and an operation to unblock my tubes I never succeeded in becoming pregnant, so he was mercifully spared the awesome task of taking me through nine months' pregnancy with all that it would have involved…

When I saw him after my return to England and gave him a letter from the doctor who had been treating me, giving details of the drugs I had been prescribed, he said, 'Jesus Christ Jack! That was a bit heavy.' It seemed that they were anti-psychotic drugs, which appeared to have had no effect on me apart from a considerable weight gain. But Daryl wasn't a happy bunny, and a new routine of more acceptable anti-depressants was prescribed and a new regime established.

And so I left Las Encinas, went to the nearest bar and ordered the best margarita I had ever tasted, caught a cab to the airport and boarded my flight to Heathrow and a very uncertain future.

11
Joel

Back in London and gratefully ensconced in the bosom of MTB, I was obviously still seriously barking – to the consternation of my friends – and now also seriously broke. So far from having returned with a fistful of dollars I was obliged to 'sign on' at the Labour Exchange, thus initiating a relationship that was to become the mainstay of my fiscal life for some decades to come.

In those days the DSS in Victoria was known as the actors' Labour Exchange – it appeared to have some understanding of the trials and tribulations of the actor's life and indeed I saw many familiar faces as I stood in the queue waiting my turn to sign on after answering the inevitable question, 'Any work in the last two weeks love?' Actors tend to avoid one another if they are not working – unemployment is viewed in the same way as a highly infectious disease, to be avoided at all costs – and even at the Labour Exchange, where we were all obviously in the same boat, acknowledgements were brief and slightly furtive, eye contact avoided as much as possible and exits hastily made. Every two weeks when my dole giro arrived I would hurry to the World's End post office in Chelsea, cash the inadequate amount the government deemed sufficient to keep body and soul together for the ensuing fortnight and take myself off to the Ritz Hotel in Piccadilly where I would sit in the cocktail bar with a glass of champagne which enabled me to face the beans on toast that comprised my diet for the remainder of the two weeks and provided me with a sustaining glimpse of the elegant world I longed to inhabit on a far more regular basis.

My fragile mental state wasn't helped by being persuaded by my lodger – I had rented a cabin to a girl called Cats – that we should leave MTB and move onto the boat next door. I had no desire to leave the sanctuary that MTB provided, but Cats had her eye on the piano: she played herself and I quite understand the lure of the neighbours' keyboard. She had also lived with me long enough to feel the need for some assistance, and the rent I would pay next door would reduce the amount she herself would have to pay. So from Cats's point of view the move had several advantages: less rent, a piano and assistance with yours truly from the two existing tenants. MTB leaked, was damp and probably the health hazard she convinced me it was; but when I left MTB I lost my home, and the boat next door proved itself a very poor substitute.

Its tenants were an American girl named Laura who was a harpist and played at the Dorchester during afternoon tea, and a chap called Campbell, a very talented pianist who also did gigs at posh hotels. The boat was called the *Lorien* and I loathed it on sight which wasn't the most auspicious of beginnings. It was modern and felt like a prefab on water. It also had a bath that wouldn't drain and a chemical loo that needed to be emptied into the 'shit boat' as it was known, which was situated further down the mooring and towed at appropriate intervals out to sea, there to disgorge its contents. Campbell was the only one of us strong enough to carry a loo containing the deposits of four adults, and as he was reluctant – understandably – to visit the 'shit boat' more frequently than necessity required, he would delay his visits until the loo was filled to overflowing, its contents clearly visible and its perfume pungent. Never having had a strong stomach and possessing a fairly fastidious nature anyway, I found the process of adding my contributions to this odious receptacle to be the stuff of nightmares. I'd had a proper loo on MTB which flushed straight into the river; and, undesirable as that may seem, I confess to longing to pollute the Thames rather than endure the horrors posed by the sanitary arrangements afforded by the *Lorien*.

Because the bath was capable of accepting water from the taps, but lacked the facility to drain it away, its contents had to be decanted into buckets, carried to the kitchen and disposed of down the sink, there being no washbasin in the bathroom. As the kitchen was situated at the other end of the boat and numerous trips were required to empty the bath, ablutions took forever, and simply keeping oneself acceptably clean became a major mission. And it proved impossible to empty the water completely; there was always a puddle of someone else's detritus to be dealt with before embarking on the procedure oneself. I'd always delighted in bathtime; lots of bubbles, candlelight, a glass of the grape and soft music playing in the background made it a sensual delight. But on the *Lorien* it became an exercise in basic hygiene only, and that was that! It was not an environment in which to indulge in sensual pleasures. When I'd lived on MTB, my neighbours Pete and Vicki's then eight-year-old daughter Emily often visited me when she came home from school. One day in response to her mother's query, 'What do you do when you go and see Jacqueline?' she told her: 'We eat chocolates and have bubble baths.' Them were good days Em, them were good days…

∽

It was F. Scott Fitzgerald who claimed that 'the rich are different,' to which Ernest Hemingway responded, 'The rich are not different, they just have more money.' I agree with both those statements; the rich *are* different because they have more money, and the rich are *not* different because they undergo the same human dilemmas we all experience. They are subject to the demands of the human condition like everybody else. However, having got my PhD in poverty I can assure Ernest that the rich – because of their money – have access to the best medical help available which enables them to either prolong life or expire in comfort. They are educated at the most private of schools. They eat the finest of foods, are surrounded by beauty (taste permitting – money itself, unfortunately, being no guarantee of taste), holiday frequently in seductively sunny climes, exercise in top-class gymnasiums with their own personal trainer, are dressed in linen, silk and cashmere and transported hither and thither in their chauffeur-driven limousines or one of those black shiny cars with the pretty yellow light on top. They do not lie awake at night as they attempt to solve the problem of how to pay the gas bill. These advantages – available only to the rich – have a tendency not only to prolong life but also to increase its quality.

The poor, on the other hand, take their place for medical treatment in the NHS queues, fingers crossed that they don't expire before their (medical) number comes up. Their education is minimal, a great deal of it gleaned from the television set whose programmes frequently give the impression of being designed to cater solely to the lowest common denominator. They live mainly on cheap, processed foods, frequently becoming obese and/or diabetic as a result. They are too often housed in the harshness of concrete estates where no tree shall grow or flower bloom. Holiday destinations rarely include the ski slopes of Switzerland or the bronzed beaches of the Bahamas. They exercise in gymnasiums where rain drips sullenly from ceiling cracks making it necessary to avoid the buckets placed strategically around the grime-encrusted floor. The changing rooms are perfumed with sweat and sadness, foot infections almost guaranteed. They are dressed in polyester and nylon, and spend hours in queues in freezing cold and sweltering heat, waiting for overcrowded buses that may or may not admit them. Or they descend into the bowels of the earth and fight for places on overcrowded tube trains, crammed against their fellow travellers in unsavoury conditions, inhaling air of dubious origins and emerging at their destination feeling either clinically depressed or inclined to homicide. Their lives contain very little quality – which also affects the quantity.

So you see Ernest, the rich *are* different, because they are *rich*. Geddit? In my experience, poverty is many things, but ennobling ain't one of them. It is time-consuming, overwhelming and destructive. It limits both choice and experience, affects every area of one's life, and is definitely no way to pass one's time on earth.

So, back to the still unsolvable question. How was I going not only to survive, but live? There is a world of difference between the two states and much as I desired to live I had no idea how to achieve that state of grace. So I continued to support the pharmaceutical industry and kept body and soul together with a combination of chemical cocktails.

One night I was invited to a party by Steven Pacey whom I'd worked with on *Blake's 7*; I'd adored Stevie on sight and continue to do so to this day. His brother Peter, also an actor (whom I likewise adored) and his wife Vicki were my neighbours on the moorings and, despite my reluctance to accept any social engagements, Pete hauled me off – still wearing my dressing gown – thinking that a few glasses of the grape and some laughs might help restore my depleted self. It was there that I met a man called Christian who worked as a colourist at Vidal Sassoon on Sloane Street. He very kindly invited me to visit the salon where he would introduce me to a stylist called Joel who he assured me would take care of me.

'I don't think of Joel as a hairdresser,' he said, 'I think of him as an artist.'

Intrigued by this description I made an appointment and presented myself at the salon about a week later. I was sitting in the cutting area when suddenly this vision appeared and I knew immediately that this was Joel. He was wearing an Issey Miyake outfit the colour of periwinkles, in a soft material. The jacket had a high collar and the effect was very Russian. He had short, spikey blond hair with black roots, magnificent blue eyes and an enviable bone structure. He was also twenty-three and the youngest ever 'art director' at Sassoon's. He introduced himself and proceeded to start cutting my hair. I was chatting away merrily when he suddenly said, 'Would you mind keeping quiet as I'd like to concentrate.' This was said in such a way that it was impossible to take offence and I have to confess to being seriously impressed by his manner and dignity.

I don't think I had ever before, and certainly not since, had my hair cut quite as frequently as I did after that initial visit. Despite the fifteen-year age gap we established a relationship, eventually becoming a 'couple'. We remained together for almost eight years, my relationship with Joel proving to be the longest I have ever sustained. Joel was a good man and true and his infinite kindness gave me the strength to continue. He alleviated my unbearable isolation and provided me with much needed protection.

A few months after we met he was asked to go to Munich and manage the salon there; I joined him after a few weeks, my joy at leaving the *Lorien* almost as great as the prospect of joining my beautiful boy in Germany! But although he had agreed to stay in Munich for two years, he found the work unsatisfying and missed the creative buzz that London provided. One day we crossed the border into Austria to visit Mozart's home and in that house of such enormous creativity made the decision to return to London. Joel also decided to leave Sassoon's and carve out a career in the world of advertising and editorial work in the fashion world which he proceeded to do with great success.

He lived a life of extraordinary glamour, constantly flying off to far-flung locations with photographers like David Bailey, John Swannell and Terry Donovan, and was surrounded by the choicest models of the day. I derived great pleasure from reading his credit – 'Hair by Joel O'Sullivan' – in all the glossy magazines and was intensely proud of him. Joel also provided for me financially throughout the years of our relationship and I shall never cease to be grateful to him for his unstinting generosity.

We both adored each other and everything we shared together was special, except for the area which had always posed such problems for me. I now understand that what I really wanted was a relationship that would provide me with protection, security and love but did not include the sexual act. Joel accepted my sexual difficulties, believing that eventually they would be resolved and we'd finally achieve the sexual intimacy we both desired to realise. But alas, it was not to be.

Five years into the relationship, I left for Africa to make a film called *White Mischief*. Forty-eight hours after arriving at the location I was stunned to find myself getting up to black mischief with an African gentleman. It would be impossible for me not to tell Joel of this liaison when I returned to England – our relationship had always been distinguished by its honesty and I knew I was incapable of keeping so great a betrayal from him. I told him the night I arrived back from location, and watching that beautiful boy's heart break was an anguish I will never again experience. To hurt so cruelly someone I loved so deeply was one of the hardest blows I have ever delivered or received and it took me many, many years to forgive myself. I'm still not sure that Joel ever has completely forgiven me, but I know it was a defining moment in his life; he lost his innocence and would never again give of himself so fully and freely. We remained together for almost three more years, but an irreparable wound had been inflicted on our union: a wound too deep to heal.

Like myself, Joel had had a childhood containing great sadness, and our empathy with each other's pain was the bond between us. He was a child of great sensitivity, born into a household incapable of nurturing and protecting that sensitivity: his parents unaware of the gifted child they had conceived, unable to recognise, encourage and develop his many gifts. His Irish Catholic parents were totally unsuited to establish a life together, and the frequent violence between them was witnessed by this small child as he pleaded with them to stop.

Eventually his mother consulted her priest; she wished to divorce her husband and knew her only hope of achieving this while retaining her position as a member of the Church was to obtain a Papal dispensation. After listening to her request the priest advised her to make an act of contrition for even entertaining the idea of divorce and to have another child. This, he assured her, would bring her and her husband closer together. She duly took his advice and a sister for Joel was born. The situation was not improved by having another mouth to feed in an already impoverished household, so his mother reported the situation to her priest, who prescribed exactly the same advice he had previously given her with exactly the same result. Another sister was born, another mouth required feeding and, thanks to the advice of the good Father, two little girls had now joined their brother in swelling the ranks of the walking wounded. The parents finally saw the light and divorced, leaving them in a state of mortal sin and excommunicated from their church.

I'm not remotely religious myself, but if a loving God does exist and presides over his flock with the care and compassion we are led to believe He does, how can His representatives on earth justify such grotesque misinterpretation of the verb 'to love'? Every religion claims to be the 'one true religion' and insists that anyone who is not a member of their particular belief is doomed to eternal damnation from the moment of death, and possibly before. It would be risible if it weren't so diabolically cruel. Religious factions constantly war with each other and inflict appalling injuries on their fellow man – physical, emotional and spiritual – all in the name of, and on behalf of, their loving God. Mind you, He hasn't done much to provide us with an image of a loving Father. Think how Jesus must have felt when told of his proposed descent to *terra firma*. There he was, hanging out with the angels sharing a spliff (I know he enjoyed the weed because Eddie Izzard says so and we know that Eddie has *the* hot line to the Almighty, so his information is impeccable), when the Archangel Gabriel floats up and tells Jesus that God wants a word. Imagine the conversation that ensued:

God: Son, I want you to do something for me.
Jesus: Sure dad; what's on your mind?
God: I want you to assume mortal form and visit Earth, son, and preach the word of God to your fellow man.
Jesus: Sure dad, no probs.
God: You will have some disciples, but not many; and one of them will betray you. This betrayal will result in your capture by the Romans who've never accepted your teachings. They will scourge and imprison you and after due consideration find you guilty of blasphemy and sentence you to death. They will place a crown of thorns on your head, a heavy wooden cross on your back and laugh, jeer and spit at you as you labour up the hill of Calvary. Once there they will crucify you, driving iron nails into your hands and feet, and a sword will pierce your side just to be sure that you have in fact pegged it. When you ask for water, you'll be given vinegar. How does that grab you, son?
Jesus: (after a long pause, and several tokes of his spliff) I'm not sure that's the best idea you ever had, Dad.
God: Trust me. Do it for me, son, 'cos I loves ya!

As far as I'm concerned if that's an example of a loving Father, you can shove it where the sun don't shine.

The Catholic Church consistently demands donations from its congregations to assist their missionaries in Africa and to provide for the poor. As the Vatican houses one of the world's largest art collections, might I suggest that it puts its money where its mouth is and flogs a few paintings which should be sufficient to meet the needs of many African countries for several decades to come? And surely it should heed Jesus's message to his disciples: pack the lot in mate, kiss the missis and the kids goodbye, and live a life of poverty and deprivation for the love of God? I've taken the liberty of paraphrasing that message somewhat, not having a bible to hand to enable me to quote directly from the text. My apologies to those it may concern... My God is Nature, which inspires in me the passion I should apparently feel for the God of religion. Awe, fear, overwhelming love and total respect. 'Ah,' I hear the God-botherers sigh, 'but who created Nature if not God?' To which I reply, 'Quite frankly my dears, I don't give a damn.' For me, God is Nature, and Nature is God, and that works for me.

Joely and I healed a great deal of each other's pain. We were friend, parent and child to each other, interchanging those roles as and when required. If we could have been lovers as well we would have found the holy grail. Three out of four ain't bad but are not, alas, sufficient to sustain a union indefinitely. After almost another three celibate years together we parted. Our journey to reach that degree of separation was painful, protracted and infinitely sad. Many tears were shed, many angry words exchanged before we were able to admit, to ourselves and each other, that our lives were no longer entwined, our futures no longer conjoined. And because the magnetic attraction that drew us inexorably each to the other had not been physical love, but an intuited spiritual and emotional empathy which inspired an experience of love that existed independently of the sexual impulse, and remained intact, our grief was great indeed.

Although I accept that our separation was inevitable and that during our time together we had lessons to both teach and learn from each other, I still question why the learning process appears to insist on great pain as a prerequisite for self-knowledge. Or is the pain caused by the Self's struggle with the self? By capital-S Self I mean the knowledge, the awareness, the integrity that already exists within all of us, but buried too deeply to be located; and by the small-s self, I mean the ego. As the ego is concerned only with its own survival and will do everything in its considerable power to retain its supremacy, and is a tricky little sod at the best of times, I can appreciate that the battle it will fight in its defence will be long, bloody and vicious, and certainly won't involve the Queensberry Rules. People who are very damaged (I cite myself as an example) tend to have large but fragile egos, I assume to compensate for their lack of any sense of Self, and come to believe that their ego *is* their Self; so when they meet with resistance to that illusion, their disillusionment is experienced as total terror. The search for the Self is doubtless the work of a lifetime – that is certainly true in my own case – and inevitably on that journey one's constant companion is pain. And I've reached the conclusion that the only attitude to have towards a lifelong companion of that ilk is compassion. The ego loses its power when presented with compassion, and one's pain is able to be integrated into the whole of the Self instead of living as a separate entity on the perimeter of assimilation.

Joel is still in my life some twenty-two years later, but he still seems unable to fully forgive me; he is convinced that my ability to manipulate is verging on the monstrous. Of course I'm manipulative – we all are, it's one of our survival tools – but what I am not is devious. My manipulative behaviour has always been unconscious, whereas once one manipulates, fully conscious of what one is doing and with a specific aim in mind, then for my money it ceases to be manipulation and becomes deviousness. The manipulator who is concerned only with his own gratification, regardless of the cost required from the manipulated, is indeed monstrous. I now understand that I manipulated others via my emotions, but the majority of my pain was expressed in the privacy of my own environment. This became difficult if I was living under the same roof for any length of time with another person or persons. Joel, because of our shared environment, was witness to a great deal of my pain during our years together; it was distressing to watch and something I much preferred to express alone because I had no wish to cause distress to others.

With the inevitability of our separation came the need to find myself another billet; we had bought a flat shortly before my African experience but there was no way I could stay there and be able to pay the mortgage. I also had no wish to remain in London; so Joel remained in the flat, and I decided to stay with friends in Cornwall.

I duly arrived in Penzance with two suitcases, four hundred pounds and a bust of a Roman Goddess.

12
Cornwall

I first went to St Ives in Cornwall at the age of nine on a family holiday. In 1953 St Ives was at its height: rich with artists and pulsating with colour and vibrancy. The small town was enchantingly pretty with its narrow cobblestoned streets and whitewashed cottages, its harbour filled with the boats of the fishermen; and a lighthouse stood at the end of the pier. Sunlight sparkled on the sea creating millions of diamond lights that danced delightedly on its surface. The soft, smooth sands played host to sandcastles; rock pools revealed tiny crabs seeking shelter from the small hands that sought to pluck them from their hiding place; buckets and spades were carried by children as they collected the myriad shells that graced the shoreline. Their parents lay in striped, canvas deckchairs, the remains of lunch in the wicker picnic-basket at their feet.

Shops with delicious aromas filled the main street and offered meat and potato pasties, fish and chips liberally doused with salt and vinegar and wrapped in newspaper, and every kind of shellfish; there were shiny toffee apples and pink candy floss guaranteed to rot the teeth; and sweet shops with Dickensian windows sold gobstoppers, penny chews, lemonade powder and saucy postcards. I was fascinated by the postcards but not permitted to view them as my father considered them vulgar.

Ladies wore sundresses with halter-necks, sandals with high heels, and straw hats with wide brims to protect themselves from the sun. Men wore white trousers, and a navy blazer over a white shirt and a suitable cravat and either a fisherman's cap worn at a jaunty angle or a straw boater also worn at a jaunty angle. That is, if they were from the South; Northerners favoured a handkerchief knotted at each corner prior to placing on the head. Paintings were on display everywhere, many of them nudes; little did I guess that nearly four decades later I would be an artist's model myself posing for the next generation of St Ives artists.

St Ives made an indelible impression on my nine-year-old self and I returned in the sixties, seventies and eighties before finally making it my home for seven years during the nineties. But when I left London and Joel, I didn't immediately make for St Ives, but Penzance. I had become close to a young actress, Siri Neal, with whom I'd worked on a children's series, *Moondial*, in the eighties. Siri was fifteen at the time and a remarkable girl: very talented and from a completely different background to my own. She lived in a small village a few miles from Land's End with her mother Lizzie and her two younger sisters, Skye and Jemima. I was invited to stay with Siri and her family soon after we finished *Moondial*. Lizzie was the archetypal hippy; her three children all had different fathers, her house was filled with friends and lovers, she was black-haired and beautiful, as poor as a church mouse, and took in lodgers and made candles to make ends meet. She smoked 'rollies' and dope and her children were beautiful, individual, well-mannered and *free* to be themselves. I stood open-mouthed at this unorthodox household and their willingness to include me into their lives.

The place they lived in was an old tin-mining village; the mines themselves had closed down years ago and their crumbling chimneys outlined against a bleak winter landscape spoke of desolation and despair. The atmosphere was that of a ghost town; its industry had been taken from it and no other had replaced it. It was a forbidding, relentless, ferocious landscape, with an undercurrent of huge passion; there was nobility in its starkness, majesty in its fury. It was elemental, primal and primitive. And I loved it!

It was during one of my visits that I took my first Ecstasy tablet. I'd always had a great fear of illegal chemical drugs and had been much too afraid to sample acid, which was the drug of choice at the time, and viewed Lizzie's suggestion that we take Ecstasy together with a great deal of trepidation. The drug had only recently found its way to England and was still in a pure state; it hadn't been 'cut' with anything and wasn't widely known or freely available, but the hippies of Cornwall had managed to secure some! This was my first experience of hippies, and I found them fascinating: their innocence, their refusal to accept the status quo, the willingness with which they supported each other, their generosity of spirit and openness of hand and heart and the richness of their lives in the areas that really matter. They may have been dirt poor but they were rich in humanity, joy and love despite the frequent hardships of their financially challenged lives.

Nobody was more surprised than I when I found myself agreeing to Lizzie's suggestion; and I can't tell you how glad I am that I did! I know that drugs can be the means of profound spiritual experiences and I have enormous respect for them. There is a vast difference between those who take them to 'get out of it' and those who view them as sacred and take them to 'get into it'. That was the approach that both Lizzie and I took and our 'trip' was truly ecstatic. We became telepathic; our energies flowed together and we became one fluid entity experiencing the dissolution of isolation, and the integrity of love.

Since that experience, which will remain with me always, I've taken half a tablet on a handful of occasions, maybe five, and under different circumstances; and I would not take it again. These days are very different to when I took it in the eighties and I would no longer trust the source. I also took magic mushrooms for the first time in the mid eighties and found they did exactly what they said on the tin. They really were magical: I found myself in a world filled with fairies, talking flowers and enchanted animals; a world cloaked in jewel colours that glowed and glittered, vivid and vibrant, oh! Such colours. I wanted to stay there forever, wanted nothing more from life than to be permanently under the influence of these magical fungi twenty-four hours a day for eternity. I've always been slightly surprised that I've only taken them less than a dozen times since, the last trip being nearly twenty years ago. And now I can't because they're apparently a dodgy combo with my prescription drugs. But offer me a 'smoke' and you'll never hear a refusal! A friend described the 'weed' to me as 'Nature's gift'. Amen to that, and fuck the begrudgers.

As I was no longer being supported by Joel and my three hundred pounds was rapidly disappearing, the need to earn money was – once again – acute. Lizzie had by this time moved to Penzance and knew a great many of the local artists. She thought I had a future as a life model and secured me a booking with a small group of artists in neighbouring St Just. I loved the work! I found it so exciting being part of someone else's creativity, able to inspire them and become their muse. What I wasn't totally crazy about was Penzance itself. There are those who are passionate about Penzance and pretty tepid about St Ives and those who are passionate about St Ives and pretty tepid about Penzance. I was certainly in the latter catagory but it was six months before I visited St Ives and only then because I was invited to.

One Wednesday afternoon I was modelling for a group in Newlyn when the telephone rang. Ken, the artist whose studio we were working in, spoke to the caller, put down the phone and came over to me. 'I've got Roy Ray on the phone, he runs a session in St Ives on Wednesday nights. His model has just called in sick; would you be prepared to fill in for her?'

I said 'yes' but somewhat reluctantly. My body was pain-wracked due to the position I was posing in. We worked in half-hour sessions and then I had a ten-minute break to allow blood to flow back into numb arms and fingers, legs tingling as pins and needles mounted a ferocious assault and feeling began to assert itself. I'd been sustaining myself with thoughts of the long, hot bath I would submit my battered body to as soon as I'd crawled home. It had been a long and difficult day and taking the bus to travel the twelve miles to St Ives was not the most cheery of prospects. But as soon as we reached our destination and I saw that enchanting little town caught in the softness of the early evening light, my tiredness left me, my step lightened and my heart lifted.

I found the studio and Roy Ray, who told me that although he ran classes for amateur painters during the summer, Wednesday night was a private session for the many professional painters who lived in the town and it met every week without fail, the only exception being Christmas Day should it happen to fall on a Wednesday. I loved the studio; it was Hollywood's idea of an artist's studio! Filled with easels and smock-wearing artists (some of them wearing berets), unfinished paintings, sculpted heads and a wooden floor liberally spattered with the paint of several generations of artists, it had a small dais in the centre of the room for the model, and a screen in one corner which served as a dressing room. It was seriously bohemian and I felt as though I'd reached Mecca; much as I love and admire them I am not a hippie at heart, but have always felt by both temperament and inclination at home in the world of bohemia.

It was the custom after the session ended to make for the Sloop Inn which sat next to the harbour on the water's edge. As I was being paid the going rate of three pounds fifty an hour I received my seven pounds, repaired to the Sloop and spent it all on drink! In winter the pub would be virtually empty except for us, and it was the bleak months of winter that I most cherished. In those days, the Sloop still had a real coal fire in the bar; its walls were hung with black-and-white charcoal portraits by Hyman Segal, converted oil lamps provided a soft light, tankards of beer sat on the long oak tables, and the air, a delicious hazy blue from the smoke of pipes and cigarettes, created an atmosphere both comforting and decadent. I knew I had to move to St Ives.

I left Lizzie and Penzance after a stay of six months, and moved several times in and around St Ives. I spent some months working at the Tinners Arms in Zennor, a pub I'd visited with my parents in the fifties. Zennor was about four miles from St Ives, situated on the moors, and consisted of the pub, the church and a small row of cottages. There were surrounding farms but the village itself was minute. I both worked and lived-in at the Tinners Arms, and with buses not reaching Zennor in the winter my one night off each week was spent on the other side of the bar in the pub. Both the pub and the church were centuries old and filled with myth and magic. A huge fire burned in the hearth in the pub, and I wished I'd worked there in an earlier century. I would have much preferred to see the pub lit by candles and firelight, filled with pirates sporting cutlasses and wearing gold earrings, with myself behind the bar wearing something fetching in crimson velvet with an artfully laced bodice supporting buoyant breasts the colour of cream. But, alas, by the end of the twentieth century we'd become a pretty drab lot.

I used to visit the church quite often and one day was discovered there by the vicar. He was a fascinating man, of Russian/English parentage; in his early forties, highly intelligent, extremely witty and refreshingly irreverent. We delighted each other and laughed a lot. I said to him one day, 'I'd really like you to be promoted, so that I can then say in all truth, "…as the bishop said to the actress".'

Serge needed a housekeeper and I was anxious to leave the pub; the landlord refused to allow me to smoke in my bedroom, an attitude which I viewed as deeply boring (besides being an infringement of my human rights), and I felt that life at the vicarage would certainly be more relaxed. When I suggested to Serge that I become his housekeeper, much as he found the idea attractive he said, 'It wouldn't work for two reasons. I have to pray four times a day and, if you were here, I know I'd say, oh fuck it, let's go into St Ives and have a lobster dinner. And it may create jealousy among some of the ladies of the village.'

How right he was! Not about the lobster dinner – that never happened – but the ladies of the village did unite to make it quite clear that I was no longer welcome in their small community. I was ignored; the subject of a great deal of gossip and even more of envy and generally made to feel extremely unwelcome, before eventually being rescued by the ringing of the telephone in the box outside the pub. It was my agent, telling me that I'd been offered another children's series by the BBC and would be required for costume fittings the following week in London. Which effectively terminated my sojourn at the Tinners Arms in Zennor. I never saw Serge again; when I next visited Zennor it was to discover that he'd left. I was never sure if it was Zennor that he'd left or the church itself.

I returned to St Ives when the filming ended; it had taken me eighteen months of moving around before I finally settled in a room above the grocer's shop in Fore Street, the main street of the town. It was a very narrow street surfaced with cobblestones and occupied by shops selling artwork, jewellery made of silver studded with turquoise, candles and new-age music, the Methodist chapel and the grocer's shop. The shop was rented by a couple from Manchester who had moved to St Ives many years earlier. Sandra and Garth (he had some Italian blood) were the salt of the earth and my landlords for the five years I lived there.

Sandra (or Sand as I called her) became a surrogate mother, despite being not that many years older than myself. She was warm, kind, always cheerful and very wise. The shop was the hub of the town and nothing passed unnoticed by Sand. She worked like a Trojan: in the shop at six-thirty to let the bread man in and on her feet until the same time at night, when she would climb the stairs to cook 'our Garth's' tea, do a load of washing, whisk round with a duster and, after finishing the washing-up, pop round to see her daughter 'our Jan' and her twin grandsons. She was definitely worth several guineas a minute.

A journalist who was gay (and subsequently became a great friend) came to town for a few days in order to interview me and the day after his departure sent me a huge bouquet of flowers. Sand looked at them, unable to believe her eyes. 'There,' she said, 'you'd never get a proper man doin' that.' Whenever John – the journalist – returned to St Ives for a visit, I would take him to see her and say, 'You remember my friend John, don't you Sand? You know: the one who's not a proper man?' Sand would blush furiously, John and I would clutch each other and howl with laughter. Wicked!

But life in a seaside town isn't all cliff walks and cream teas. Small towns are rife with gossip: everybody knows everybody else and there's very little to do out of season, so a heightened interest in the lives of others dominates during the remaining nine months (the season being only a brief three). I'd become rather reclusive, and when I did venture out to do some essential shopping preferred not to have to speak to anyone; so I wore a disguise of dark glasses, a black hat with large brim pulled low on my forehead, red lipstick and a mink coat (this was in my more unenlightened days). As nobody approached me I assumed my disguise was effective; it was some years later that a friend told me that, far from being effective, everybody knew it was me and had many a good laugh at my idea of anonymity.

Cornwall was healing for me, but my depressions gave me little respite. Very occasionally I would go to London to do a small and not very exciting job, but in the main I was unemployed and totally without funds which in itself is a tad depressing.

I had great friends living in Kildare in Southern Ireland. I went to spend my fiftieth birthday with them and they made it very special for me. They even had a *Sachertorte* sent over from Demels, the famous coffee-shop in Vienna; flowers arrived from friends in England and I had a very jolly time. But when I returned to my room in Cornwall, despair wrapped itself around me as I looked at my life thus far, and how little I had achieved. I was fifty years old, penniless, unemployed. I had no husband, no children, no immediate family, my home was one rented room, and I was completely alone. I had contributed nothing and could see no purpose to my life. What was its point? Why was I here? How had I failed so spectacularly to utilise the great potential of my youth? And for how much longer could I continue to live with a pain that never left me?

~

It was while I was in St Ives that Alan Bates re-entered my life. We had remained in touch since *Otherwise Engaged*, saw each other occasionally and spoke, also occasionally, on the telephone. When I read in a newspaper that his wife Victoria had died, I wrote to him and received a phone call from him a few days later. He was coming down to Cornwall with the ice skater John Curry and said they would drop in and take me out to tea, which they duly did. Al and I then went for a walk (John, feeling tired, having decided to take a nap in the car); and it was during that walk that both of us became aware that the attraction that had always existed between us was about to take wings.

Some years later, after his death, I attended his memorial service and one of the speakers, Alan Bennett, told how Bates was always falling passionately in love – with either sex – and then panicking and spending the remainder of the (usually brief) relationship trying to extricate himself from it. This was echoed by Simon Gray in his diaries and was certainly accurate in my own experience. After a flurry of increasingly passionate phone calls I went to stay with Al in London prior to leaving with him for a Greek island where he was due to receive an award. I was included in his inner circle who, like myself, all appeared to think that a marriage proposal would take place in a suitably romantic setting on said island. And he did indeed take me to an incredibly romantic setting: a candlelit restaurant overlooking the sea, the sky thick with stars and a huge moon spilling a silver light on the water. But far from expressing a desire to make an honest woman of me, he dumped me. I was distraught.

I was in the grip of a romantic fantasy and Bates – in his day – was the romantic hero of so many films. He first found fame in *A Kind of Loving* in the late fifties, a seminal film taken from the book by Stan Barstow. Then followed many others: *Women in Love*, *The Go-Between*, *Far from the Madding Crowd*, *Nothing But the Best* to name but a few. He was stunningly beautiful, seriously sexy, and desired by both men and women. And he himself was attracted to and had relationships with both sexes. The reason I mention this is because homosexuality in the late fifties and early sixties when Bates shot to stardom was still illegal. This alone made it necessary for him to conceal his homosexuality; and coupled with his status as a sex symbol it became imperative. But when I met up with him in the early nineties the situation had changed dramatically; homosexuality had long been made legal, the secrecy surrounding all matters sexual had long been shattered, and Bates was almost sixty.

Personally I think Bates's feelings where women were concerned were deeply ambivalent. We were necessary to present as a front to his public, because we confirmed his public image as a sexy, heterosexual male; and the unvarnished truth, as I see it, is that in 1992 the public couldn't give a fuck. Those days were long gone; and yet, despite his hugely successful later career playing character parts, he was unable to let go of his image of himself as the romantic leading man of his day. But I don't think he liked women; I sensed his deepest feelings for them were fear and rage. And I wasn't in love with Alan the man, but with the characters he'd played. In my head, he was Mr Rochester and I was Jane Eyre (not that he ever played Mr Rochester nor I Jane Eyre, but it had long been my favourite book) and on my first visit to London to stay with him, I arrived at Paddington station wearing a cape and clutching a recently purchased Victorian travelling case which was intended to be transported on the back of a coach and four and was totally unsuited to travelling by train in the twentieth century. Alan was completely unable to raise it from the ground despite several valiant attempts; a trolley was required to wheel it to the taxi rank, and I was less than popular with himself. He couldn't understand why I hadn't used a rucksack. Nobody played the romantic hero better than Bates in his day, but off screen he was remarkably unromantic, although I doubt that he was aware of that himself. And since (as I now understand) I was in love with his 'reel' life, as opposed to his 'real' life, the shit was bound to hit the fan when the whole house of cards inevitably collapsed.

After leaving our Greek island we were travelling to another to join Simon Gray – one of Alan's closest friends – and his wife Victoria. Alan's way of dealing with unwelcome emotional situations was to withdraw from them. I found this very difficult as he would advance and then retreat, constantly pulling the rug from under my feet. He would confirm his love for me and then become emotionally unavailable, sometimes for several days. I cried a great deal; Alan was remote and I'm not convinced that we were the liveliest house-guests Simon and Tory could have wished for, although both of them were sympathetic to my obvious distress and very supportive.

Our two weeks in Greece finally limped to a close and we returned to London. Alan went to Derby to visit his mother, and I to Cornwall to lick my wounds. In total, the intense period of our relationship lasted a mere three weeks, at the beginning of which I believed we would marry and at the end of which I knew we wouldn't! Being dumped is never a cause for celebration, and being dumped at fifty definitely something to be avoided. I sank into a massive depression from which I took many months to recover.

Believe it or not, we resumed our relationship a couple of years later. I had gone to London to appear in a previously unperformed Arnold Wesker play at the New End in Hampstead; Al came to see it, took me to dinner after the performance and suddenly we were back on track again! He came to St Ives to stay with me several times after the play closed but inevitably the pattern repeated itself. The relationship continued until I finally returned to London for good; Garth and Sand reached the end of their lease on the shop and decided not to renew it, so I had to choose to remain in Cornwall without them, or return to London and attempt to revive my career. I chose the latter.

I rented a tiny flat in Holborn from a friend, and found work as a life model at various art schools in London. One afternoon I was doing a gig at a college that had never used a life model before and the facilities, or lack of them, made for a pretty grim experience. It was freezing cold, I was lying on bare floorboards and consoling myself with the prospect of dinner that evening with Al. 'Wouldn't it be wonderful,' I thought to myself, 'if I finished this gig, left the building and found Al waiting outside ready to whisk me home in the warmth of his car, and not have to battle with the rush-hour crowds on the tube?' I then thought, 'What the fuck am I doing here, lying stark naked on a filthy floor in order to earn five pounds an hour' – the London rates being higher than the Cornish – 'when I have a millionaire beau who claims to be in love with me?' That night over dinner I finally ended the relationship. When he was awarded his CBE I wrote to congratulate him; I started the letter, 'Dear Alan Bates CBE' and signed it, 'Love, Jacqueline Pearce DSS.' He then telephoned me: 'Darling, what does DSS mean?' Bless.

So, after spending a total of seven years in Cornwall and approaching my fifty-seventh birthday, I returned to the metropolis, hoping against hope to effect a return to the ranks of working actors, earn some money and finally put an end to the monotony of poverty.

13
London – Part One

I returned to London after an absence of seven years and remained there for a further nine. The smallness of the flat in Holborn which I initially rented from friends was more than compensated for by its location; I could walk to virtually anywhere, and there was a wonderful market at the end of my street – I've always loved markets. And it was great to be in close contact with friends whom I had only been able to see infrequently during my Cornish years. But I'm not really a city girl and I missed the call of the sea, the wildness of the moors, the wind in my hair and the freedom I had known in St Ives.

I had also started a relationship with a (much) younger actor – Richard Hansell – whom I had worked with in a play which we performed at the Dublin Festival. It was a two-hander based on a true story about an incestuous relationship between a mother and her son. Although it was quite sexually explicit, the Catholics of Ireland were extremely tolerant and our three-week run was very well received. It was quite demanding vocally and involved a fair amount of shouting, crying and general angst. There was a bug doing the rounds and, at the end of the second week, I developed a sore throat. I was able to work with it, so foolishly didn't consult a doctor. When we closed a week later my voice gave out completely and didn't return for about ten days; and, when it did, it was without my top register. Despite attempts to regain it, I am still without it to this day.

I developed a lot of respect for Richard when we were working together. He was a very talented painter as well as a wonderful actor; highly intelligent and blessed with an irresistible sense of humour. He was also twenty-seven years younger than me. We didn't become lovers until some time after the play closed; and although it was destined to end – we were at different stages in our lives – we stayed together for two years and to this day remain the closest of friends. The flat I was living in belonged to Richard and his sister Louise; and, after I had been there for two years, Louise required the flat to live in herself. I spent quite some time at the Homeless Persons' Unit attempting to get myself into some council accommodation which would have proved permanent and affordable. I was spectacularly unsuccessful in my quest. I was single, childless and English; this was at the time when immigrants seemed to go straight to the top of the queue despite the mutinous mutterings of the home-grown. There were numerous notices on the office walls asking applicants to refrain from abusive outbursts and attacks on staff. I was eventually offered a room in a friend's house which saved my bacon in a major way.

During my two years in Holborn I did a one-woman show at the Edinburgh Festival; it was based on experiences in my own life but, despite the good reviews and four stars it received, was one of my least enjoyable experiences. I didn't really know what I was doing and felt far from comfortable doing it. What I in fact wanted to do was 'stand-up' but had no idea how to approach it. The piece was devised, not written, and I wasn't at ease with the material despite having supplied it myself. It was quite revealing and I think it was that that disturbed me. I didn't want to bleed in front of an audience, to expose myself in that way; and for what end? I felt diminished, not enhanced, by the experience and I left as broke as when I arrived – the idea having been to make some dosh. We (the director and myself) didn't lose any money, but only managed to break even. The audiences seemed to enjoy it but I was not a happy bunny and seriously relieved when it was all over.

The same director then called and asked if I would be interested in playing *Shirley Valentine* in a tour around India. The idea of playing Shirley greatly appealed to me. It was a wonderful part; I was not obvious casting, and that in itself was exciting; and the prospect of touring around India as well made for a lot of icing on a very delicious cake. My cup ranneth over.

There was one slight problem. The contract was still being finalised: did I accept before signing on the dotted line, which was the only way to give myself sufficient time to learn the part, and take the risk that it might fall through? I decided to take the risk. I had, and needed, three months to learn it – it being a two-hour monologue – and once I'd finally got it under my belt Spencer (the director) suggested that I do a performance before we left for India, in front of an invited audience, which would give me the opportunity to see how it played. I thought this an eminently sensible idea and we booked the Tristan Bates Theatre for the occasion. We were leaving shortly after Christmas and the performance was booked for Sunday December 20th which happened to be my fifty-fifth birthday. (I was too old to play Shirley but somehow managed to get away with it; or so I was assured by kind friends after the performance...)

And, guess what? The contract fell through... So my first and last performance took place on the same night. The theatre was full of mates including Simon Gray, Alan Bates and Arnold Wesker; and, despite seriously questioning my sanity in the dressing room (how the *fuck* did I manage to get myself into this situation?), I confess to having enjoyed myself when I finally got on stage. And I was thrilled when Al said to me later, 'I probably shouldn't say this Jack, but whenever I go to the theatre, no matter who I'm going to see, I always find myself drifting off at some point during the performance. But I never left you for a second, you held me completely.' Gosh! I consoled myself with this thought when I signed on the following morning.

Inevitably, this singular success was followed by a serious depression. My insecurity was present and frequently dominant in every area of my life – except where the work was concerned. I never doubted my talent, but frequently questioned why I had it. This great gift was also the greatest of curses. Being unable to express myself in the only way I knew how, being cut off from my own (my fellow actors, my tribe) and unable to find any other outlet for my massive internal energy resulted in unbearable frustration and an agony of mind that I cannot allow myself to remember. The only identity I had was that of 'actress'; deprive me of that and I was left with an intolerable sadness which was too painful to endure. (I continue to refer to myself as an actress, despite it being 'politically incorrect'. Apparently we're now all 'actors'. That being the case, why are there categories for both 'actors' and 'actresses' at awards ceremonies? For purposes of identification, that's why. I am female, and therefore an 'actress', and delighted to be so!)

I longed for the release of death. The pain which dominated my life was no longer supportable; I emerged from the savage despair of depression, weakened in both mind and body. 'You can't afford to get into these states, Jackie,' Hop said to me one day. I was very aware of that, sunshine, but what I seemed unable to do was prevent them from happening. They had become something far greater than myself, and my resistance to my despair was diminished with every claim it made on me. And try as I might, I could find no reason to continue living. Despite my best attempts to heal myself I was in constant pain. As I looked back on a lifetime of loss, rejection and deprivation, I could not help but be aware how fragile my hold on sanity had become.

In a session with Hop one day, he suddenly said: 'Jackie, what would you say if I suggested to you that perhaps, on another level of reality, before you assumed your physical body, you knew what your life would involve and you chose this experience?'

I stared at him for several moments. 'Hold it right there, sunshine. Are you telling me that not only did I have the childhood from hell, the effects of which are still with me to this day – because my childhood defined my life, as it does for everybody – and despite my very best efforts to change the data that was pre-programmed into my personal computer at an age when I had absolutely no control over what information went into it, and which I'm still having a massive struggle to delete from my hard drive; and not forgetting the depressions, endless disappointments, poverty and despair that have been my lot for the past few decades... are you telling me that *I chose this*? What kind of a schmuck am I?'

Hop's approach had changed over the many years of our relationship, and this was during what I think of as his Buddhist period. I was not impressed; I could see no reason for any sentient being to voluntarily choose a life of suffering. Particularly as my suffering seemed so barren. I didn't emerge from a depression feeling that I had gained in wisdom and emotional maturity – far from it: I was weakened and enfeebled, and the knowledge that I would inhabit that hell again and again a source of nightmares.

I considered suicide virtually every day and knew it was a valid option – my 'Get Out of Jail Free card' – and yet, despite the many occasions when I sat in front of a bottle of pills, the contents in my hand, I never took them. What prevented me from doing so? I must have had an awareness on some deep unconscious level that I would survive the horror that my life had become; but, being understood only on that unconscious level, it was of no comfort to me. I should make clear that there were also periods of huge laughter, good times with friends when the depressions lifted; but I knew always that they would return, and that awareness cast a shadow over the good times. I could never be completely free of it.

FROM BYFLEET TO THE BUSH

I still had no idea who I was, or what my roots were. My father rarely discussed his childhood and he only ever mentioned my mother in the most negative of terms; once when I was laughing he said, 'Don't laugh like that Jacqueline, it reminds me of someone else I used to know.' Late one night when I was about fourteen he came into my bedroom, crying. 'Don't ever let me down; I was let down by a woman once before, and I couldn't take it again.' As well as knowing nothing positive about my mother, I felt as though I spent my childhood trying to prove to my father that I wasn't someone I had no recollection of ever having met.

I sent a friend a few chapters of this book to cast his eye over. He emailed back questioning my choice of the words 'childhood from hell', and suggested that kids dodging bombs in back alleys in Beirut were in fact the ones having the 'childhood from hell'. I saw his point, of course, but was unable to agree fully with it. Hell is the result of loss, and the child in Beirut who loses its entire family and knows the terror of living constantly with an acute awareness of death is indeed in hell; but that child growing up in Byfleet, struggling to survive the loss of her mother with no suitable substitute and experiencing a total absence of love, was also in hell. Hell is hell no matter what form it takes; does either child have firm foundations on which to build their adult lives? No, of course not. A firm foundation comes from the security of knowing you are loved; of never doubting that you have a right to be here. Our childhoods define the remainder of our lives and, as most people's lives have involved inadequate parenting, very few have the security provided by a loving childhood – and those that do are blessed indeed.

☙

I moved in with Vicki whom I had first met when I lived on my houseboat. She had then been married to Peter Pacey, but had recently separated from him after over two decades together. Their two children, Oscar and Emily, had moved with her. Em was now studying at St Andrews University and

Oscar was completing his pre-uni education from home. I spent my first sixteen months in the spare room, longing for the day when the tenants in the basement moved out and I could move down there. The basement flat consisted of one large room, with a separate – large – kitchen and a reasonably sized bathroom. It had French windows that opened onto a tiny patio with steps leading up to the garden and, best of all as far as I was concerned, a *fireplace*! I longed to sit in front of it; to be tucked up in bed at night watching the flames flickering in the hearth providing the only light in the room. When I finally got to move in I did just that; and the morning I drew back my curtains to discover swirling snowflakes falling onto an already white landscape I was in heaven. The comforting warmth of the fire, Caspar (cat) curled up next to me on my bed, Cyril (squirrel) eating his breakfast of nuts on the window sill and the white wonderland outside combined to form the stuff of fairy tales and I wanted it to last for ever!

I think the mistake that Vick and I made was deciding to live under the same roof. We're chalk and cheese and our differences were inevitably going to cause friction. Vick is a graphic designer and the house was her dream home. It was a five-storey affair in a terrace built in 1895; it was also in an appalling state and needed everything doing to it. I respond to every environment I'm in, and I found the endless chaos and clutter in the house extremely depressing. It was also colder than a witch's tit in winter, but it bothered Vicki not a whit. The house was completely lacking in comfort: five storeys and nowhere to be comfortable. I thrive on comfort and cosiness; Vicki is a stoic and seems to court discomfort. I could never understand why she didn't simply make one room comfortable while the exterior work was being done. The interior, which Vicki regarded as 'cosmetic', could only be done after its completion. That took almost twenty years...

I'd been living in the house for about six months when something wonderful happened. I auditioned for, and was offered a part in, a new production of a J. B. Priestley play,

Dangerous Corner. A month's rehearsal in London, a month at the Yorkshire Playhouse and then... into the West End! I was walking on air and couldn't wait to meet the rest of the company and start rehearsing.

And when I did, it took me no time at all to recognise that I had lucked out in a major way. They were all seriously talented and very beautiful; three boys and three girls. Well, they seemed like boys and girls to me, as they ranged in age from nineteen to thirty and I was fifty-seven. The boys were Rupert Penry-Jones, Steve John Shepherd and Patrick Robinson; the girls were Dervla Kirwan, Anna Wilson-Jones and Katie Foster-Barnes – I adored them all. And in character and temperament, all so different. Rupert had a wonderful honesty; you always knew where you stood with him which suited me down to the ground. He was also passionate about the work, gave very good 'notes' and insisted that the standard that had been attained by Laurie Sansom – our director – be maintained after we had opened and Laurie had departed for pastures new. Not that there was any real danger of it dropping; we were all totally committed to the show.

Ru was also immensely kind (a quality I find irresistible) and a complete gentleman, and if I had been thirty years younger his life wouldn't have been his own! He's a bit of a hero to me is Rupert P-J. Some people find him arrogant, but he's not at all; he doesn't suffer fools gladly – why should he? – and I think his seeming arrogance is part of the persona he has assumed to protect a great sensitivity. When he discovered that I was spending Christmas on my own (which I really didn't mind) he said his parents would love me to join them and, after making sure that it wasn't an act of charity to save the 'old dear' from a solitary Christmas, I duly went and had a lovely day with all the P-Js and Dervla.

They were kind enough to invite me for the following two Christmases which were spent at their home in Anglesey in Wales. A beautiful, warm, comfortable, cosy home overlooking the sea with an Aga in the kitchen and a roaring log fire in the sitting room. Mum (Angela Thorne) was a wonderful cook – we always had a fantastic fish pie on Christmas Eve – and she and Dad (Peter P-J) were amazingly generous hosts.

Ru said to me one Boxing Day morning, 'You're not like a guest.' He was called away before I had time to ask him what he meant and I forgot to ask him later, but I did give it a lot of thought and it was only years later (since I've lived in Africa) that I think the penny finally dropped. Prior to staying with the P-Js I'd only ever stayed with friends of many years' standing who knew that I never appeared before lunch, always wore a dressing gown and rarely left the house. The P-Js, however, were completely unaware of this; it never occurred to me to warn them and I had no idea how eccentric my behaviour must have appeared to them! On Christmas Day everyone sat at the lunch table dressed in their Christmas finery and I would be in my dressing gown. But I always wore my pearls with it for a special occasion, which for me constituted being dressed up. The reason for such seeming eccentricity was because I could never see the point of dressing if I was at home as I'd only have to get undressed again in order to go to bed, and as I spent as much time as possible *in* bed and clothes have never really interested me much anyway (costumes on the other hand *fascinate* me), why bother? So I didn't. However, when I was at the P-Js I wasn't at home, and I think that is what Ru must have meant by his remark. I do hope they understood that because I felt so at home with them, I could behave as though I *were* at home, and that my behaviour was not the result of appalling manners. It's quite sobering to think that I may have caused massive offence without even being aware of it.

I fell in love with Steve John Shepherd on sight; it was impossible not to as he was breathtakingly beautiful. Curly hair the blue-black of a raven's wing, merry brown eyes, enviable bone structure, perfect teeth and able to make me cry with laughter. When I discovered he'd renamed the play

Dodgy Bend I fell about for a fortnight. When he let slip that like me he was addicted to Radio 4 I proposed on the spot. And this was before the read-through.

I had a particular affection for Pat Robinson as I've never made any secret of my soft spot for the 'brothers'. We talked endlessly about every subject under the sun and enjoyed each other's company enormously. I thought casting a black actor was inspired on Laurie's part; it provided an extra edge to the piece, and like Ru and Stevie he was beautiful to look at.

Dervla Kirwan was gentle, gracious, exquisitely beautiful, reserved and very private. I had first seen her in *Ballykissangel* and was very impressed by her talent, so was delighted to find myself working with her. Before rehearsals started I had heard negative reports about her from friends of friends who had worked with her. She was reputed to be difficult, ruthlessly ambitious and to be avoided at all costs. Nothing could have proved more inaccurate. She was (very) generous both off stage and on, kind, obviously vulnerable and sensibly desirous to protect that vulnerability. I can only assume that rumours like the one I just referred to are started by those of vastly inferior talent and beauty and are the result of that malign emotion: jealousy. Fuck 'em.

Anna Wilson-Jones was also beautiful: cheekbones that hove into view fifteen minutes before the rest of her face, huge eyes and a stunning figure. Anna came from a medical family and was training to become a doctor herself before abandoning her studies to become an actress. Her father was a vet, and her three siblings all doctors. They were a seriously intelligent family, and Anna's formidable intellect coupled with her beauty and talent made for an awe-inspiring package.

Katie Foster-Barnes was nineteen and the youngest member of the company. It was her first job: she took it completely in her stride and proved wonderful in the part. Katie-kins (as I called her) was a Sagittarian like myself, her birthday being on December 19th, the day before mine. Katie-kins was very laid-back; nothing seemed to faze her and she became very dear to me. When we went to Leeds for a couple of months prior to coming into town, flats had been arranged for us and all we had to do was choose who to share with. Pat (typical 'brother') decided to go it alone, which left Ru and Stevie to share. As Katie and I were both smokers and Derv and Anna non-smokers, Katie-kins got the short straw and had to share with the elderly lady. She was extremely gracious about it. She also had no objections to me having the en-suite with the larger bedroom; I have to admit she arrived in Leeds to find me already ensconced, but said she would have insisted I have it should she have arrived earlier. I was so thrilled with my suite. Wall-to-wall carpeting, ample storage space, a space-age bathroom and *warm*! After the chaos and discomfort of Vicki's, I was in heaven.

We blotted our copybook with Nica Burns, our producer, very early on in the production. Laurie was staying in her flat for the rehearsal period in London and invited us all back after the read-through for a drink so we could get to know each other. (Nica was away at the time.) We arrived at the flat clutching bottles of bubbles, and proceeded to become very merry very quickly. Alas, we ran out of bubbles (I think there was an 'offy' nearby but we were all too pissed to get there), so we explored our surroundings and were delighted to discover some bottles secreted in the cellar. We all looked at each other, decided Nica wouldn't object in the least (and we would certainly replace them anyway), and popped corks with gay abandon. Little did we realise that they had been given to Nica and her husband on their wedding day and were being saved to drink on their tenth anniversary. We were informed of this at the next rehearsal, felt suitably ashamed and hoped that 'champagne-gate' wouldn't count too heavily against us.

We were at the West Yorkshire Playhouse one afternoon a few days after we had opened when Stevie suddenly erupted into the green room, mobile pressed to his ear. 'There's been a terrorist attack on the World Trade Centre,' he shouted. 'My Dad's on the phone and he's watching it on television; people are jumping out of windows and one of the towers has collapsed!' We stared at him, open-mouthed, unable to comprehend what he was telling us. Slowly the horror of the event hit home; we looked at each other, too dazed to speak. We had no television or radio so were unable to get a clear idea of what had happened. How could this be? The World Trade Centre in New York had been the subject of a terrorist attack? It was unbelievable; the enormity of the attack impossible to comprehend. We left the theatre and walked into a world that was as shocked and stricken as we were. It was a very subdued company that took to the stage that night and a very subdued audience that we played to. I felt as though I were living in a nightmare; the world had changed irrevocably and horrifically and assumed the unreality of a sci-fi disaster.

We returned to London, opening on November 7th; and the press night proved to be a bit of a disaster. Laurie and our designer had devised between them a spectacular *coup de théâtre* in the second act, involving an owl flying into and smashing a glass window. It was scrupulously rehearsed before every performance by our totally efficient stage manager, and had always produced the desired effect on the audiences in Leeds. But on opening night in London, it didn't work... The cast waiting for their cues backstage looked at each other in bewilderment, made their entrances and soldiered manfully on to the end of the show. Despite protestations from members of the audience after the performance that it really didn't matter we knew that, of course, it did; and our post-show party was somewhat muted as a result. Our reviews were mixed and not what they should have been and our houses affected (as were theatres all over the West End) by 9/11. We closed after three months and I was sad to leave that wonderful company who had shown each other such support, camaraderie and respect.

From that production resulted two marriages: Rupert and Dervla, and Stevie and Anna; and two children have been born to each union. Laurie told me that now when he's casting he says to those auditioning: 'We may not make it into the West

End, but you will find true love!' I was asked to be godmother to Steve and Anna's first daughter but was later fired from the position due to a misunderstanding which has – unfortunately – yet to be resolved. But time is a great healer and I am optimistic that the love between us will ultimately triumph and normal harmony will be resumed at some time in the future. They were both such wonderful friends to me and I regret so much the rift that I seemed to have caused which no amount of heartfelt apology has been able to heal. I have treasured memories of that production and those precious people who were my playmates for seven months.

14
London – Part Two

The play had closed; I was finally ensconced in my basement flat and all was well with my world. I had made a great friend of Caspar – Vicki's cat – which didn't go down too well with Vick. She accused me of enticing him away. It is impossible to entice a cat; independent creatures that they are, they make their own decisions. It was simply that I offered better facilities. Like me, cats love warmth; and Caspar, it being winter, decided that curling up on my electric-blanketed bed, or in a chair in front of the fire, was a far better option than freezing his balls off upstairs in the arctic cold that pervaded Vicki's quarters. But it certainly resulted in a definite frostiness in Vicki's attitude toward *moi*.

The need to earn money was (as was customary) occupying my thoughts somewhat, when something quite miraculous occurred. I received a letter from my cousin Peter informing me that if I contacted him, I would hear something to my advantage. I immediately did so and was told that a very distant and previously unknown relative had died intestate in Singapore. The executors of his estate had performed extensive searches to locate any surviving family members and, as one of the beneficiaries, I was to receive the sum of sixty thousand pounds! My jaw dropped; I was unable to absorb this wondrous news. I'd gone from zilch to sixty grand in a matter of seconds. I was rich! When I finally recovered the power of speech I telephoned all my nearest and dearest to share this amazing stroke of good fortune; they all knew of my long association with poverty and I knew they would be thrilled for me.

It took some months before the money finally arrived. The day it hit my bank, I stood at the teller's window and withdrew twenty-seven grand – in cash – which I had agreed to loan to my godson, who was standing by my side, and gave it to him. His flat was on the market and he would repay me as soon as it was sold. I never doubted for a second that he would pay the money back: he was my godson, both his parents were dead and we were extremely close.

I was also in a position to celebrate my sixtieth birthday with a party; what joy! The champagne flowed, I was surrounded by loving friends and my heart was full indeed. A matter of weeks later another very close friend approached me and borrowed a total of fifteen grand, which he would be in a position to return three months later when he had remortgaged his flat. It never crossed my mind that, as both my godson and my friend were unable to borrow from their respective banks, perhaps I was being a touch foolhardy to advance them the money myself. It also never crossed my mind that neither of them had any intention of ever repaying me, until it became apparent that that was indeed the case. My friend's flat was repossessed, as was my godson's (something he didn't tell me); and I had lost a total of forty-two grand. I had paid off a lot of my debts; the party didn't come cheap and I'd also made a gift of a few grand to another friend in need. So my fortune had rapidly dwindled and I had no one to blame for my stupendous stupidity but myself.

It wasn't so much the loss of the money that emotionally felled me; it was the huge betrayal by two people I loved dearly whose only intention had been to exploit my naiveté and gullibility for their own ends. I had also just missed out on appearing as a contestant in *I'm a Celebrity, Get Me Out of*

Here. That this also felled me is an indication of the depth of the madness that now had me in a vice-like grip. Now that I am relatively sane, and nothing on God's earth could induce me to appear in the aforementioned programme, I can only thank my lucky stars that I came second, having been pipped to the post by Jenni Bond. But as I say, I was not the most rational of bunnies at the time and it was a heavy blow indeed.

I was able to recover the money from my godson with the aid of a friend, who was very large, very black, sported a completely bald head and felt very protective towards me. No blood was spilled, no threats were made; but my godson did agree to sign a document drawn up by my lawyer to repay the money over a period of twenty-four months, the amount being deducted at source from his pay cheque and sent on to me. I have never seen my godson from that day to this. Because the money was returned to me in small amounts instead of a lump sum, I neglected to put it in the bank and for two years lived like a proper person and enjoyed myself thoroughly. The fifteen grand has never been repaid, and the betrayal I felt plunged me into a doolally of a depression which lasted for around nine months. After taking an assortment of anti-depressants, none of which provided any relief, my doctor finally hit on a winner and forty-eight hours after first taking it I was free of depression for the first time in almost nine months. Two weeks later I was diagnosed with breast cancer. Stress doesn't cause cancer, but it can cause it to kick in. I cannot help but conclude that the stress I experienced as a result of those betrayals provided the spark to ignite the cancer that manifested as a result.

༄

It was while I was receiving treatment for Carol (as I called my cancer), and nine months after I had made him the loan, that I terminated my ties with my godson. When I was initially diagnosed he was the first person I called, but when I discovered that his flat had been repossessed and learned the full extent of his manipulation and mendacity I terminated the relationship.

When I went to see my oncologist to be given the news re Carol, I had been a non-smoker for three months. Giving up smoking in the midst of chronic depression probably wasn't the best time I could have chosen, and from my previous attempts to kick the cigs I knew that after three months there was a strong likelihood that the craving for a fag was about to become particularly virulent. So when my oncologist said, 'I'm sorry to have to tell you, Miss Pearce, but I'm afraid there is some cancer,' my immediate response was, 'Fantastic! I can have a fag.' I felt completely exonerated of all responsibility. I had cancer; I could be staring into the jaws of death in the very near future. Who could possibly begrudge me the comfort of a fag in such a situation? Certainly not I... I left the hospital, rushed into a café, bought a coffee and a packet of ten and haven't looked back since. Strength of character never was my strong suit.

When Vicki arrived home that evening she came down to my flat to ask what the doctor had said. She opened my door to find me puffing away and grinning happily to myself. I told her I had cancer. She looked at me as though I were mad.

'But why are you smiling; you've just been diagnosed with cancer?'

'Because I'm not depressed,' I beamed at her, 'and if I'm not depressed anything else is a breeze. If I had been diagnosed two weeks ago when I was still depressed I would undoubtedly have gone irretrievably insane and come to a very sticky end, but now I'm up and running it really isn't a problem.'

And, compared to depression, I found cancer a walk in the park. It was when I realised that I was ill with a potentially life-threatening disease and money was once again tight, and I was owed forty-two grand by two people who had not and were not making any effort to help me in my time of need, that pennies finally began to drop.

Vicki and I had several drinks as I planned how to deal with any difficulties presented by chemotherapy. I was in the fortunate position of being able to pay someone to do the shopping, whisk round with a duster and carry in the coal which would enable me to languish in bed and not impose on others in any way.

'The one thing I refuse to be,' I said to Vick, 'is a burden to my friends.'

'But you've always been a burden to your friends,' she informed me. My hysterical laughter reverberated around my kitchen for several minutes.

Needless to say I was filled with anxiety to think that I was a burden to my friends and discussed it with Mo (one of my oldest and dearest friends) at our next dinner *à deux*. I can rely on Mo to 'tell it like it is' so her opinion was very important. She thought about it for a moment.

'No, you're not a burden in any way. There have been times when I have been very concerned for you, because I knew you were going through a very difficult time and I was powerless to help. But that is not being a burden, that is being concerned about someone you love.'

I then asked Jan, another old friend, who confirmed everything that Mo had said and also said I was a 'great joy'! It was also suggested that perhaps Vicki's remark, as well as being ill-timed, revealed a certain antagonism towards me which was probably rooted in jealousy. Some years later Vicki admitted to being jealous of me, but I was at a loss to understand how anyone could be jealous of a late-middle-aged woman who was unemployed, constantly broke, a lifelong depressive, unmarried, childless and barking, a mass of unfulfilled potential and totally frustrated. But it seems that she was. There's nowt so strange as folk.

After two operations to remove the tumour and my lymph nodes I reported to St Thomas's Hospital for my first session of chemotherapy. I was accompanied by Dervla and Anna and so touched by their support. I was collected from the flat, sat with during the treatment, fed cappuccino after it, and deposited on my doorstep afterwards.

I had a great curiosity where Carol was concerned; I found the whole process of treatment, hospital visits and everything involved with my treatment quite fascinating. I never knew a moment's fear, and any residual fears of death I may have harboured disappeared completely, never to return; and to be free of the fear of death results in a great personal freedom. I had never found depression interesting, but Carol interested me greatly. That's not to say that chemotherapy doesn't have its difficult moments; the side-effects aren't a laugh a minute and I wasn't sorry when I finished the treatment six months later. My oncologist told me later that they had treated my cancer 'very aggressively' so I'd been given a very heavy dose of chemo which had obviously been very successful. Whether my attitude to the possibility of death would have been different if I had been a married woman with children, grandchildren etc. and all the accoutrements of family life is of course a moot point, but I think that any fear I may have felt in that situation would have been for those I loved and how they would survive their loss, not for myself. Grief, of course, that I would be leaving them; but a fear of death itself – I don't think so.

During treatment, I gave a great deal of thought as to how I would celebrate its ending. A holiday in sunny climes appealed to me: one of those cruises around the Med surrounded by witty, elegant fellow travellers, engaging in sophisticated conversations with erudite companions, champagne cocktail in hand, dolphins leaping gracefully and frequently by the side of our jolly yacht, appealed to me enormously. But it appeared that a Saga cruise – the only kind I could conceivably afford – would be filled with geriatrics and possibly lacking the style I was looking for, which apparently was extinguished during the 1950s and unlikely ever to return.

So... what else? A cruise down the Nile which would take in the Pyramids also appealed. I could wear white, beautifully cut trousers with a silk shirt – also white – and a wide-brimmed straw hat trimmed with silk roses in a delicate shade of palest pink to protect myself from the burning rays of the sun. I would be surrounded by intrepid native bearers who would ensure my safety should we encounter marauding companies of crocodiles looking to nab a light lunch. We would glide through narrow stretches of river whose banks were thick with dark green foliage which reflected onto the water and cast deep mysterious shadows upon its surface. I always imagined making this trip alone, but the cost of hiring a suitable boat, plus attendants, for one person was prohibitive in the extreme so also had to be dismissed as a possibility. As did a houseboat in Kashmir, a palace in Venice and a tour of Russia in a troika. The decision I came to eventually couldn't have been more removed from my initial imaginings.

I was in bed one night, propped up on a pile of pillows, gazing at the fire and pondering my still-uncertain future. I had just come through a life-changing experience – and yet my life hadn't changed at all. And I *wanted* it to change. Totally. I was no longer prepared to spend my time trying to understand the reasons for the failure I undoubtedly was; I needed to reverse that mindset into one a little more life-enhancing and less demanding. I knew that I had always done the best I could in whatever situation I found myself in; but, as my attempts to become bigger than my wound still defeated me, I had to seek solutions in other ways – although I hadn't the slightest idea how to achieve that.

I was also no longer prepared to continue with what passed for my career any longer. I would no longer wait for a phone call from my agent, which rarely came, and when it did was to give me details for a cattle call for a commercial, attendance at which I found demeaning, humiliating and degrading. Because treated as cattle we undoubtedly were; and I think my barely concealed hostility towards the entire process must have communicated itself on some subtle level to the clients, because I never, ever was cast in one! I also wasn't interested in auditioning for any more crap parts in seriously shallow afternoon soaps or to suffer the ongoing rejection that inevitably is part of an actor's life. It was time to face facts and acknowledge that I'd fucked it, big time, completely sabotaged myself; and as offers of good work with good people rarely materialised – four years had elapsed since *Dodgy Bend* – I had no alternative but to steer myself in another direction. But what direction? There must be something I felt a passion for other than acting, the search for which had eluded me for many, many years. I turned my head and looked at Caspar who was curled up on a cashmere cushion (fashioned from a moth-eaten sweater of mine), purring contentedly in front of the fire... and suddenly it happened! The light-bulb moment that flashed into my brain with the impact of a Mack truck. Eureka! Of course! *Animals!*

I was passionate about animals. I knew there and then that my immediate future lay with them. But what animals? Primates: they had always fascinated me, so why didn't I do some volunteer work with primates? Being a confirmed Luddite I had always avoided the 'Google' button on my laptop, believing I lacked the ability to use it successfully; but my finger clicked the button and before I knew it the Vervet Monkey Foundation in South Africa appeared before my eyes complete with photographs of enchanting monkeys. I was hooked. Due to my IT ignorance I thought this site was the only one in existence; I failed to notice the message at the bottom of the page that this was pages one to ten out of a possible selection of trillions of others. I have since had cause to be extremely grateful for that ignorance. My time at the VMF proved not only to be the biggest adventure of my life, but to change its course forever.

15
Africa

I'd done it! I'd booked myself in for two months to work as a volunteer at the Vervet Monkey Foundation in Limpopo, South Africa. I say I'd booked it, but as I'm still incapable of sending an attachment without taking my laptop into the shop – I kid you not – I was able to rely on the skills of a friend who arranged everything for me. I then received an email from the VMF with a list of essentials I would require for living in the bush. I was going to be staying in a tent in what was called 'Tent Village'. I scanned the list and thought it must be written in a foreign language as I recognised very few of the words. What the fuck was a rucksack? And hiking boots? (I was the only person at the VMF to carry a handbag and wear ballet shoes.)

A friend guided me into shops I had never dreamed existed: camping shops where I purchased, among other things, a miner's lamp, a rucksack – which, even though it was pink, my favourite colour, I was completely unable to bond with – huge boots – which I never wore – and safari-type trousers with zillions of zips which would enable me to wear them full length, three-quarter length or as shorts, and which were stolen from the washing line shortly after my arrival. I'm not sure I was ever really able to conform completely to bush dress code, but with a few adaptations I managed a reasonable proximity; I was happy and my fellow volunteers frequently hysterical with laughter at my attempts to look casual.

South Africa was a country I would never have visited if I hadn't taken the decision to work with monkeys. I'm not sure why, but I didn't consider it to be really Africa; as though it was a sort of sanitised version of East Africa, which was obviously the 'real' Africa. And of course there was the appalling history of apartheid which had tainted the country for me. How wrong I was! But the beauty, magic and mystery of that vast country still lay ahead of me. I had no idea how affected I was going to be by SA: how she would claim my soul, release my spirit and enable me to achieve the integration I had sought for so many years. How the desolation and despair that had crippled me would be replaced by joy, peace and overwhelming gratitude that my love of life had triumphed over my yearning for the oblivion of death. But that still lay in the future.

Most of my friends were convinced that I wouldn't last twenty-four hours and would doubtless be on the first plane home once the reality of life in the bush presented itself. Despite that I had a jolly dinner party the night prior to my departure. Stevie (Steve John Shepherd), who as well as being outrageously beautiful is also a brilliant cook, said he would cook for us all and arrived mid afternoon laden down with pots and pans, exotic ingredients and rich red wine and proceeded to start chopping and peeling. Stevie had been going through a difficult period where the work was concerned and need a break ASAP. He had been waiting to hear about a telly that would have provided that break, so his disappointment on hearing that it hadn't worked out was acute. He had been told shortly before he came over to prepare dinner, and to have still come when all he wanted to do was howl his anguish to the heavens was indeed above and beyond the call of duty. Fortunately the tide turned for him soon after that massive disappointment and his star was on the ascendant once again.

Eight of us sat down to a delicious dinner and lots of rich red wine and bubbles. And despite believing that I would be back by the weekend my friends all gave me presents; one of which delighted me like no other. It was a rucksack! 'Gosh!' I said, 'how lovely.' I was actually in shock as the givers were dear friends of many years' standing who knew me very well, and I would have thought a rucksack was the very last thing in the world they would make me a present of. I was instructed to open it which I duly did and – lo and behold! – it contained a complete picnic set that wouldn't have been out of place in an Enid Blyton book. It had cups and saucers and plates, containers for milk and sugar, a flask for champagne or ginger beer, cutlery and gingham serviettes. It was the campest creation I had ever encountered and I adored it. I couldn't wait to use it and immediately saw myself in a safari suit and ballet shoes producing my rucksack at the end of a long day's elephant-trekking and offering my fellow trekkers chilled champagne and canapés from my elegant picnic hamper.

I'd had a brief and unhappy affair shortly before leaving England. The man involved had managed to devastate my self-esteem and confidence to a quite spectacular degree and I was still feeling fragile when I began my journey to the dark continent. I was also terminally exhausted by all the preparations involved for my departure. I arrived at Heathrow to check in to discover that no more aisle seats were available and I was therefore to occupy a middle seat which is my idea of hell. I also have a rather weak bladder which necessitates frequent trips to the lavatory, and the prospect of having to climb over sleeping fellow passengers – it was a night flight – was enough to make me dissolve into a paroxysm of weeping which continued unabated as I boarded the aircraft. My seat was next to one of the largest men in the world and the thought of having to clamber over him numerous times during the flight the stuff of nightmares. I continued to weep, a fact which was studiously ignored by the passengers on either side of me, until I was rescued by a kindly flight attendant who led me to a vacant seat in the front row. It was still a middle seat but with enough leg room in front of it to enable me to leave my seat without disturbing my fellow passengers. My relief was overwhelming and the flight passed in a haze of alcohol and sleeping pills.

I arrived at Johannesburg airport early the following morning and was met by a relative of a friend with whom I was going to stay the night and who had booked me a ticket on the bus for the five-hour journey to Tzaneen. I boarded the bus the next morning and watched fascinated as the urban sprawl of Jo'burg was replaced by vast stretches of bush; black townships with dwellings that appeared to be held together by blu-tack and sellotape and heat that steadily increased as our journey progressed. We stopped for a break after travelling for two-and-a-half hours; I left the bus for a much-needed fag and was hit by a blast of hot air as the doors opened. The closer we became to our destination the higher the temperature rose. Tzaneen is sub-tropical and proved to be very hot indeed. The final hour of the journey was very beautiful as we wended our way through mountains, their peaks hidden by hazy clouds through which the sun was unable to penetrate fully. They appeared ghostly in the fading light of late afternoon but also emanating an energy of immense power.

I was met at Tzaneen bus station by Josie, the volunteer co-ordinator, and driven the thirty kilometres to the sanctuary; we turned off the main road and drove into the bush for the last two or three. We arrived at Tent Village and Josie said I had a choice as to which tent I would prefer as three were available. I examined all three and was somewhat concerned as none of them had a functioning zip, the flaps being held together with some extremely fatigued velcro. I chose the most efficient-looking velcro and my bags were thrust into the tent's interior without further ado as the light was almost gone by then and Josie needed to show me the layout of the village. This included two outdoor showers and two eco-loos which were also outside and proved to be large holes at the bottom of which were millions of worms devouring human waste at a prodigious rate, which they then excreted and transformed into an efficient fertiliser. I think that's what happens anyway. A lavatory pedestal and seat were placed over the top of each hole.

Unfortunately, if the wind was blowing in the wrong direction when one was attempting to eat breakfast in the open-air kitchen opposite, the location of the eco-loos meant that their aroma made for a highly effective appetite suppressant. Although the loos themselves were concealed by a surround of thatch, it proved impossible to disguise their perfume except for the blessed occasions when the wind favoured the occupants of Tent Village.

In those days the sanctuary was still establishing itself and the village contained about fifteen to twenty tents. Less than five years later it has evolved into a large complex of wooden cabins and Tent Village is no more. It was a very special time for all of us who experienced it and will remain forever in the hearts and memories of those who did.

I was then taken up to the house – about a ten-minute walk from Tent Village – which was owned by Dave du Toit, one of the two partners who had founded the sanctuary. We took lunch and dinner there and also our recreation; there was a pool table in the room next to the kitchen, and a very well-stocked bar – no wine unfortunately – which did a roaring trade with the volunteers.

I was taken into the kitchen and introduced to my fellow volunteers (about fifteen of them) who were already having dinner, and sat down. The meal was vegetarian sausages, chips and baked beans, with a huge bowl of salad should one wish it. As I looked at my companions for the next two months – the average age was around eighteen – and the total chaos of the kitchen, seeds of doubt regarding the wisdom of my decision began to surface. I opened a cupboard door and was unable to avoid the rats' droppings surrounding the condiments or the accumulated grime that was ingrained on every surface. I would never describe myself as a candidate for the 'Dora Domestic Housewife of the Year' award, but this was unlike anything I had previously encountered. There had also been a contaminated-water scare shortly before I arrived which meant all our drinking water had to be boiled before use. The water was boiled in the same enormous saucepans that our food was cooked in, and what was presented to us was definitely tinged with the vegetable oil that had been used to cook many, many meals. It was also lukewarm.

After dinner, I was accompanied back to my tent by two very kind fellow volunteers. I opened the velcro and saw the interior properly for the first time. It wasn't pretty. There was a pool of still-to-be-identified water on the floor, several large toads and a two-inch-thick piece of foam rubber over which had been placed a threadbare sheet of dubious cleanliness. A plastic bedside table completed the décor. My new friends removed the toads and wished me a good night's sleep.

I sank onto the foam rubber, which was a mistake as getting up again proved to be quite daunting and could only be accomplished by assuming a kneeling position on all fours and hauling myself upright using the plastic table for leverage, a procedure which occupied the best part of ten minutes. I unzipped my vast travel bag and groped around for the set of miniature whiskey bottles I had – on the advice of a friend – purchased duty-free at Heathrow. I rarely drink spirits and have never been attracted by whiskey but right then it had all the allure of mother's milk. I downed a bottle only for it to hit my bladder with the force of a ten-ton truck, meaning that a visit to the eco-loo was urgently required.

I reluctantly parted the velcro, and stepped into the pitch black of the African night. Despite an almost full moon, thick cloud obscured any light it would otherwise have afforded. I was unable to get the hang of my miner's lamp, which seemed to have far more functions than a simple on/off switch, and stumbled off in the direction of the eco-loos. I was then enveloped by a huge and very thick spiderweb which was woven between two trees, and emerged from my struggles to extricate myself sweating profusely and weeping copiously. I finally made it to the loo where I not only peed for England but also managed to drop my miner's lamp into its murky depths.

After the nightmare return to my tent, I groped around for some candles which I knew I had packed, panicked because I couldn't find them and threw the contents of my bag hither and thither before finally grasping them in my hot little hands. I lit one, sank once again onto my two-inch mattress, crawled into a sleeping bag for the first time in my life, downed another miniature of whiskey and sobbed my heart out. I had undoubtedly made a massive mistake; my friends had been right, and I wanted nothing but to be on the next plane out of the hell in which I landed myself.

Suddenly the flaps of my tent flew open and a large creature thudded onto my chest. When I recovered consciousness, which I briefly lost, I found myself being nuzzled by a wet nose and my face covered in very wet kisses from a hot tongue, which belonged to Candy, one of the dogs who lived at the sanctuary. Never, ever had I been so grateful for the warmth and companionship of another living creature. Candy remained my constant companion until her death sixteen months ago, and I loved her passionately.

The reason I didn't leave the following morning was simply that I was too exhausted. I continued to cry and remained in my tent for most of the first three days, venturing up to the house when I felt it might be reasonably clear of fellow volunteers. I was alone in the kitchen on my second night when an extraordinary man suddenly walked into the room. He was roughly my age – early sixties – and had long silver hair pulled into a band at the nape of his neck, piercing blue eyes and a fierce face, with high cheekbones and deeply tanned skin. He was around six feet tall and had the body of a much younger man. He exuded charisma and I found him quite beautiful. We looked at each other. 'Hello,' he said, 'you must be Jackson, I'm Arthur.' This was Arthur Hunt, Dave's partner and the man who actually looked after the monkeys.

'Yes,' I replied, as the tears rolled down my face.

'Why are you crying?' he asked.

'Because I'm in a lot of pain,' I told him, 'and I seem unable to heal myself.'

He smiled at me very kindly before saying, 'Perhaps the monkeys will heal you.'

In an attempt to regain some kind of control over my emotions I went outside and met a young Afrikaans boy called Rudi who had a very close bond with the monkeys and could imitate their sounds so accurately that his ability to communicate with them was the stuff of legend. He held my hands and said, 'The monkeys told me you were coming; they said you were a special one and I was to take care of you.' The moon was full, the scents of jacaranda, camellias and bougainvillea floated softly on the still night air, creatures of the night called to each other and the mystery and magic of the bush ignited a flame of recognition and longing deep within me.

The next morning I finally went to work with the monkeys. It was cold and cloudy and rather damp when I reported for duty at eight a.m. I was introduced into the baby enclosure which housed thirteen babies aged between four and five months. They all had to be given their bottles of milk, and Sandy who was introducing me asked if I would like to feed one myself. The bottles are usually placed in the gaps in the wire of the enclosure, but Sandy gave me a bottle and handed me a tiny monkey whose name was Felix despite being female (in Afrikaans, Felix is a girl's name). She lay in the crook of my arm and gazed at me with eyes that seemed to contain the wisdom of the world. She placed one tiny hand on the neck of the bottle and curled the other one around my finger. Her eyes never left mine, and by the time she had emptied the bottle she had claimed my heart completely. And although I didn't fully realise the impact that my love for this magical creature would have on my life, a bond had been forged between us that was deeper than any other I had ever experienced.

We worked on a rota system, and when I discovered that night at dinner that I was scheduled to work the next day in another enclosure and not with the babies, my hysteria knew no bounds. 'But I have to be with the babies,' I cried, 'I have to be with the babies!' As I had already established myself as dangerously disturbed at best and seriously insane at worst, the organisers decided that discretion was the better part of valour and I was allowed to remain with the babies for the two months of my stay.

At the end of my third week I found myself in the grip of a severe bout of 'traveller's tummy'. An eco-loo in the bush is not perhaps the ideal place to find oneself in this condition, and living in a tent in thirty degrees of heat not perhaps the ideal environment in which to recuperate. I wanted to die and the sooner the better. And until I did I wanted a proper bed, a flushing loo and lots of TLC.

When it was finally over a week later I had dinner with Arthur and he invited me to become a long-term volunteer. This would mean that I would no longer have to pay to be there; I would be given my food and tent but no salary as every penny went towards the monkeys. What I thought was, 'Are you out of your fucking mind?' What I said was, 'May I think about it?' The man was obviously as deranged as I was, but it was a generous offer and I wouldn't want to hurt his feelings.

The long-termers, as they were called, were a core group of about seven volunteers. They were usually in charge of one of the outdoor enclosures where troops of monkeys were living. In order to do this they had to establish themselves as the head honcho of the troop. Monkeys don't distinguish between themselves and humans; as far as they are concerned a human is a fellow monkey, and in order to lead a troop that human has to know he/she is recognised as the leader of that troop. They have to be the alpha male/female. Adult monkeys can do a great deal of damage, and should the handler not have absolute authority over the troop it could prove extremely dangerous. And because they are working with wild animals there is always the element of risk, of the unpredictable.

I was in no way alpha-female material. The babies thought I was great but would beat me up as soon as look at me when they became young adults. I had no authority over them whatsoever; I was good for cuddles and grooming, but very little else. Long-termers are there for one reason and one reason only: their passion for the monkeys. Most of them had been there since the sanctuary was formed and their commitment to, and care of, the monkeys was humbling to behold. I had enormous respect for them; all young kids, earning nothing and giving their all to the monkeys in their care. Quite why I had been invited to join the ranks of this talented, dedicated group of monkey-handlers was a bit of a mystery (to them as much as to me). I shared their passion, but could in no way match their youthful vigour and physical strength.

But it seemed that my ability to relate to the babies and the sick monkeys would prove to be of value. A sick monkey needs a lot of one-to-one care. This requires a great deal of time, and I was the obvious person to fulfil that role as I lacked the physical strength to clean enclosures and dig fire-breaks. I did clean the enclosures initially, but one day Sandy found me on the verge of collapse as I scrubbed out an enclosure in thirty degrees of heat. My face was puce, my heart about to explode and my legs quivered like jelly as I attempted to stand on them. I was subsequently relieved of the heavy work which meant I had the time to give to the sick and injured, which I felt was a far more intelligent use of my assets.

I had one-and-a-half days off each week and I used them to go to the Lodge. Most of the volunteers went there during their time off as it had a pool, restaurant and bar, and air-conditioning in the rooms. I would stay overnight, revelling in the coolness of my room, the large bed, flushing lavatory and room service. 'This is the life,' I would tell myself. I loved every second; if it wasn't for the fact that I missed my monkeys so much, it would have been perfection.

As my second month at the sanctuary progressed, my attitude towards my life there completely changed. I fell in love with it all! Living in a tent; my fellow volunteers; the chaos in the kitchen; the sheer joy of living surrounded by nature; the excitement of thunderstorms with spectacular lightning; rain beating down on the fragile canvas of my tent as it clung to its precarious moorings; the freedom; the fun; the dogs; the bush; the sunsets; the view of the moon and stars from the window of my tent; and most of all… the monkeys. And because the sanctuary was still in its infancy, and nowhere near as established as it is today, there was a frontier feeling in the atmosphere; we were pioneers establishing a trail for future travellers to follow.

By the end of my two-month stay my devotion to my babies was total; I knew each one by name and was fascinated by their individuality, their intelligence and curiosity and their emotional responses and needs. I became their mother and my job was to give them the security and stability they needed in order to survive in the wider world, and at the same time try not to humanise them too much – a difficult task. When monkeys reach maturity at around four years of age, they naturally reject the humans they have bonded with; nowadays human contact is kept to a minimum which makes the process of separation much easier for both human and monkey, but five years ago when the sanctuary was in its infancy and knowledge of their needs less developed than it is today, hands-on contact was much greater. And although minimal human contact is far better and less traumatic for the monkeys, there isn't a handler who doesn't cherish their memories of those days and the intimacy they experienced with the monkeys in their care. My favourite time with them was midday when the sun was high in the sky and the air very hot. All thirteen of them would somehow manage to find a part of my body to hold on to and then they would fall asleep.

Felix always dived down my top and her tiny face would gaze up at me as she nodded off. I would have monkeys on my head, my lap, clinging to my legs and poking out of the pockets of my shorts. When they woke up about forty minutes later and cased the joint for something to snack on, I would be covered in pee and poo and blissed out. It wasn't all sweetness and light: frequently fights would break out between them – usually over food; fists would fly, blood would be spilled and screams would rend the air. Mine!

I loved every second of my time with my babies. And as the date of my departure drew ever nearer I came to realise and accept that my future lay here, in this magical land with these magical beings who had so completely claimed my heart. How could I leave these monkeys who had come to trust me? How could I betray that trust by leaving them?

I went to Arthur and accepted the position he had offered me. I would return as soon as possible after I had resolved my commitments in England. Other volunteers were introduced to the babies before I left, so they would be used to other handlers and have some continuity of care. Monkeys, like us, vary enormously in temperament and character. I learned to recognise the vulnerable ones: the ones who had seen their mother shot or run over – had witnessed the brutality of the world around them and who would find find themselves unable to survive in it for long. Their huge vulnerability – their naked need for warmth, protection and security – mirrored my own and provided the means to enable me to connect with these wild animals on a spiritual level. This connection is, to me, the greatest of all privileges. To feel at one with a wild animal, to be trusted enough to be admitted into its world, is an awesome experience.

On my final day at the sanctuary I took Felix with me as I left the enclosure for my coffee break in Tent Village. She sat on my head as I joined some fellow volunteers at the table. One of them looked at me. 'You're sitting in the African bush, drinking coffee with a monkey on your head? Not many people can say they've done that.' Ain't that a fact, and how lucky am I to be one of them? I looked at Tent Village, at the washing lines we'd rigged up from which hung brightly coloured knickers, socks and towels all flapping their 'hellos' in a welcome breeze; at the tents which reflected the personality of the occupants, and at my fellow volunteers. I listened to the chattering of the monkeys in the enclosures behind me, looked at the bush that surrounded me and my heart contracted with the knowledge that all too soon my life would be lived away from all I had grown to love and discover in the power of this mystical land.

Quite how I thought I was going to achieve my objective of making my home in the bush, it never occurred to me to wonder. That I had no inkling of the difficulties that would be placed in my path before I was able to achieve my objective is definitely just as well…

16
Beating About the Bush

I was intoxicated by Africa; seduced by the bush, the monkeys, the myriad people I lived with, the lushness of the nature that surrounded me, the profusion of frangipani and bougainvillea that filled the air with their scent, the vastness of the landscape, the majesty of the mountains and, above all, the overwhelming sense of euphoric freedom that flooded my being and flowed from me, bringing with it a profound sense of joy and gratitude. That's not to say that life didn't have its little ups and downs because of course it did. Except at the sanctuary they were never little ups and downs: they were always major, bloodletting dramas!

There was a core group of volunteers who lived, worked and played together on a daily basis. The long-termers, as opposed to the short-termers who came and went, lived at the sanctuary. As well as their place of employment it was also their home for some considerable time, usually several years. It was a small community even when it was full, averaging I would think around thirty volunteers, both long- and short-termers. So in such a small, enclosed community, the occasional personality clash was surely to be expected.

The place was seething with jealousy, rivalry, intrigue and passionate attachments which would inevitably explode with volcanic force leaving any survivors licking a great many wounds. I was frequently the trigger for these eruptions, only realising it when I was caked in volcanic ash and gasping for air. Sandy, who was fifty when I arrived, had been there for two years and was in love with Arthur. When she confessed her feelings to him and and asked what she should do, she was met with a succinct 'Leave'. She remained, and still carried a brightly lit torch for him when I rocked up over a year later. Sandy became convinced that Arthur had fallen in love with me, told him that he had her blessing should he wish to marry me, wished him love and peace – and wished me dead from that moment on. I remained in blissful ignorance of the green-eyed monster festering with animosity as she skilfully disguised it and proffered friendship.

The intensity that came with living at the sanctuary was highly addictive; it was stimulating, exciting, demanding and exhausting – an adrenalin trip for junkies. Sandy was a lovely person: a Buddhist, a therapist, warm and very kind. But when she erupted she turned into Jack Nicholson's character in *The Shining*. She had a contretemps with Arthur one sunny Sunday afternoon, and I suddenly heard these blood-curdling screams coming from the direction of her tent. Sandy had a large axe and was hacking with ferocious savageness at a large tree stump (which I suspected was a substitute for Arthur) as she screamed her rage and vented her spleen. She calmed down eventually but I knew I never wanted to upset her. So when I discovered her duplicity and was told of her obsession re myself and Arthur I wasn't completely sure that I wouldn't be discovered one morning slain in my sleeping bag.

Not long after that she decided that she was going to leave the sanctuary, which she proceeded to do, leaving a letter of explanation for me to give to Arthur after she had departed. She had fallen out big time with Rudi a couple of weeks previously and issued an ultimatum to Arthur: 'Either he goes, or I go.' When Rudi failed to leave she then made the decision to leave herself. I suspect she was hoping that having made this grand gesture Arthur would finally realise her worth – she was also brilliant with the monkeys – and ask her to return. But she had seriously miscalculated Arthur's response – or lack of it – and, as I knew she would, regretted for some years her decision to leave the sanctuary and her monkeys. Sandy had worked with her troop for three years by this time, and had established a very close relationship with her guys. When she told me she was leaving I was afraid for her and tried to persuade her to stay. I knew what those monkeys meant to her and that her heart would break once the reality of leaving them really hit home – as it did. Arthur, I felt, was very unforgiving and despite her repeated requests refused to allow her to return. But she had alienated his partner Dave as well so the decision was not entirely his.

With Sandy's departure there were seven remaining long-termers. Eighteen-year-old Rudi was as camp as the row of tents in which we lived and the only Afrikaaner amongst our number. Indy, also eighteen, was Afro-English with a honey-tinted complexion and African hair and a source of endless fascination to the blacks with whom we lived. Ryan, another eighteen-year-old, was born in SA and lived there for the first few years of his life before moving to Northern Ireland from whence his parents hailed. He had, to me, an almost incomprehensible Northern Irish accent which, coupled with the effects on his brain of his vast intake of drugs from a very tender age, made him an interesting character to say the least. Lornie clocked in at nineteen, was English and boasted a body resembling Dawn French's before her recent metamorphosis into a sylph. Lisa, twenty-three and English, and Vicky, twenty-six, also English and from a very good family in Norfolk, were the oldest of the youngsters. Which left me, aged sixty-two, bringing up the rear and unquestionably the oldest member of this outstandingly eclectic and indeed eccentric group. It shouldn't have worked, but somehow it did.

Initially I was extremely popular and lovingly welcomed into their midst. But due to the volatility of the relationships between the others this proved to be the honeymoon period before I fell completely out of favour. Indy and Ryan were on-off lovers before they finally split and Ryan hooked up with Vicky. Vicky and Indy had been best mates as were Rudi and Ryan. Indy was not best pleased to see Ryan (whom she still fancied) fall for Vicky, and Rudi then bedded Indy and fell out with Ryan as a result. At the time I was having a cement foundation laid for the garden shed I was intending to move into and had moved my tent during the interim onto the patch occupied by Rudi – who was now living with Indy – it being the only space large enough to park my rather large tent. Lisa replaced Indy in Vicky's affections and I became aware of a definite *froideur* toward myself. I was completely puzzled by this until it was explained to me that I was expected to side with one or the other of these warring couples. As it was absolutely nothing to do with me, taking sides had never occurred to me, but – as I was living next to Rudi and Indy and having a very good time with them – the assumption on the parts of Vicky, Ryan and Lisa was that I had allied myself with my new neighbours and rejected the other three in doing so. In consequence, I was sent to Coventry. Every two weeks the long-termers had a committee meeting with Dave and Arthur, and when I stood up at the next meeting and said that I was appalled to have been sent to Coventry by a group of teenagers, my popularity reached an all-time low.

Four years later, Vic and Ryan are still together, Lisa is married and the mother of a young son, Rudi has also married and I understand Indy is still breaking hearts on several continents. So all's well etc. I'm still in touch with those kids; a bond was forged during those years at the VMF which despite – or perhaps because of – all the dramas, will keep us linked for a long time to come. I had some of the best times of my life with those guys.

Vicky was also a brilliant handler and was in charge of the troop in the Goliath enclosure. All the enclosures were named after monkeys, and the monkeys who ended up in the open-air Goliath enclosure were the ones considered too emotionally damaged to ever be integrated into a troop. It takes months and sometimes years to achieve integration and success is never guaranteed. But Vicky's success was pretty much total. Her extraordinary patience with the monkeys in her care, her devotion to their welfare, was humbling to witness. She was also very beautiful with long, thick, auburn hair that hung almost to her waist. Her integrity marked her out as being very special and her friendship was (and is) very important to me. Vic taught me a great deal about the monkeys, and when we worked together we established a very good rapport which could only benefit them as they are completely aware of the emotional equilibrium of their handlers.

Indy was another gifted handler, as well as being incredibly skilled in almost any area of life that you care to think of. She had trained as a ballet dancer and was talented enough to become a professional, had run for the county on several occasions and was also an adept horsewoman, and several career options were open to her. But then she had an accident which permanently damaged her knees and those options were no longer available. Indy was as effective at self-sabotage as I had been, and was still grieving for those losses when I met her. She was also in the mainstream academically and had the street wisdom of an alley cat!

Indy and I adored each other and recognised, and were quite awed by, the similarities of our mutual insecurity. Like myself, Indy was riddled with it and it manifested as a constant demand for attention. She was insatiable in her need for love, couldn't get enough of it; had unrealistic expectations of her fellow man and had become emotionally stuck. I was looking at a mirror image of myself. And what an essential step in my evolution would that reflection reveal itself to be. At eighteen years of age Indy was one of the wisest beings I have ever encountered. She understood when insecurity and fear overtook me: when the earth fell from beneath my feet and I was hurtled into a seemingly endless space which was barren of support and provided no protection, and would howl like a wounded animal. Indy greatly assisted me in finally freeing myself from those all too frequent confrontations with what I can only conclude was my own insanity.

The biggest difference between us was that Indy was consciously manipulative and played people like puppets on a string, whereas I only ever did so unconsciously; so Indy decided to give me instruction in the arts of manipulation and street wisdom, which she considered essential to survival. It took a while but pennies finally began to drop and I was awed by this child who made Machiavelli look like an amateur! But it seemed far too much like hard work to me; all that plotting and planning and scheming and remembering required to engineer a situation to suit your purpose. So I continue to use the direct route, although she has taught me to recognise when someone is attempting to manipulate me – I think; although I still need to work on my gullibility.

It appeared that among the criteria for acceptance into the sanctuary was the desire to have as little to do with the 'real' world as possible. We were each in our own way some kind of fugitive from reality, and the less we had to do with it the happier we were. This included Arthur who had dropped out of mainstream society many years earlier and was a law unto himself. He had either lost or never had any of the official documents required by the SA authorities to prove that he did in fact exist; and had no intention of acquiring any. I don't think it was 'reality' that we were all intent on avoiding, simply the massive, petty bureaucracy involved in being legit. We were all living with the irresponsibility of teenagers and having a ball.

Entertaining at the VMF was a formidable task. All necessary crockery and cutlery would have to be hauled down from the house to the tent of whoever was hosting the event. Food would be cooked on an open fire and guests would stagger up clutching bottles of wine, beer and several bottles of spirits. The amount of alcohol consumed at the sanctuary was prodigious. I watched amazed as these teenage kids held drinking competitions, downing shot after shot of hard liquor preceded by numerous bottles of wine, both red and white, and cases of beer. I never joined in these competitions as I have an inbuilt cut-off point. I feel sick if I drink more than three glasses of wine and have to take a break before continuing. Having said that, with a determined amount of practice I did manage to achieve a pretty respectable alcoholic intake; although I always stuck to wine, with maybe an ice-cold beer at the end of a shift, which after a day of working in searing heat tasted like nectar from the Gods. (Dave eventually bought an ice-making machine which cheered us up enormously until, inevitably, one of the volunteers managed to break it.)

Because wine wasn't stocked at the sanctuary, I consoled myself temporarily with vodka and tonic when I first arrived. One night I saw some volunteers heading down to their tent with a bottle of dry white which they had bought in town. 'But how can you drink warm white wine?' I asked, aghast at the prospect, 'and from a plastic glass!' All the main fridges and the cooker were gas-powered and seriously ineffectual. Ice was unheard of (this being long before we got the ice-making machine) so all drinks were warm, with the exception of beer and mixers which were housed in small fridges powered by electricity. To drink warm white from a plastic glass was, I felt, a prospect too ghastly even to consider. Due to my remarkable capacity to adapt I was drinking dry white, at blood temperature, in a chipped tooth mug before the week was out.

Being of the same generation, Arthur and I gravitated towards each other and became very close. When we first met he looked as though he had been cut off from his fellow humans for a very long time. Wild-eyed, dressed in shorts and a shirt that had long since seen better days, unkempt and dishevelled and sharing his one-roomed cottage with scores of monkeys – which proved unsanitary and unhygienic – he could have given Robinson Crusoe a run for his money. But when I finally coaxed him into clean attire, a shower and a shave, I have to say he did brush up exceptionally well. But that was a process that didn't occur overnight. At that stage Arthur had very little to do with the short-term volunteers having become decidedly misanthropic over the years. All new groups of arrivals would receive an introductory talk from Arthur explaining how the sanctuary came into being, what his aims were and his opinion of the human race. Although he was a very good speaker, eloquent and with an attractive speaking voice, his assertion that human beings were nothing to do with the animal kingdom but had arrived from another planet and were a separate and vastly inferior species did tend to lose him some of his audience who could only conclude that he was barking.

Arthur's cottage was also serving as a sick bay; so when the day came that a new and vastly superior sick bay was finally available, and a wooden cottage built next to it for Arthur, it was indeed a day of great celebration. All the people from Tzaneen who supported the sanctuary by making donations of food for the monkeys and all the local dignitaries were invited; a ribbon was cut; and Arthur's rehabilitation into the suave and sophisticated fellow that emerged from a very dodgy chrysalis was finally set in motion. He began mixing with all the volunteers, showing up at parties given by the long-termers and rapidly proving himself to be the proverbial life and soul.

In those early days at the sanctuary a great deal of grass was inhaled, Arthur lighting up at six a.m. and disappearing at regular intervals for a surreptitious puff throughout the day. He called grass 'nature's way of saying hello'. It was of course absolutely verboten as many of the volunteers, myself included, arrived via one of those agencies that specialised in placing people in projects they wished to assist. As smoking the weed is illegal in SA it could only harm the sanctuary if some snotty-nosed short-termer arrived home and spilled the beans to mummy and daddy who would lodge a complaint with the agency, which would then threaten to sever their contact with the VMF if this practice wasn't terminated immediately. So smoking had to be covert; but frequently wasn't. The odour emanating from Arthur's cabin – despite his liberal application of room spray – tended to give the game away.

Those days are, alas, long gone. The survival of the sanctuary and the welfare of the monkeys is paramount and these days the VMF is squeaky-clean and run far more efficiently as a business than in the days of yore.

Sandy's conviction that Arthur was in love with me was not without foundation. He certainly loved me, as I did him, and we did discuss marriage (long after Sandy's departure); but rather half-heartedly as both of us had broken marriages behind us and couldn't see any real justification for following a conventional path for which neither of us was really suited. The situation we had was ideal: we lived near to each other but maintained our own households and personal space. We had both companionship and privacy. However, both of us being outrageous romantics, the idea of plighting our troth deep in the bush with monkeys in attendance did have a certain appeal. Little did I know that when I said goodbye to him in March 2008 I would never see him again.

During the first fifteen months of my life at the VMF I had stayed twice on a three-month automatic visitor's visa and once for six months when I able to get an extension at the local department of Home Affairs. In one of my trips back to England I discovered that I no longer had my home in Kennington. Vicki was distraught but her elderly mother – who had *always* insisted that she would *never* want to live in London – was going to have to come whether she liked it or not. She was rapidly losing her marbles; Vicki was receiving telephone calls from her mother's irate neighbours and had no option but to bring her to London and look after her. Her mother made no resistance to this proposal, being able in her more lucid moments to recognise that she could no longer continue living in the country on her own. So far, so good. But the only place that Vicki could house her… was in my flat. I had nowhere to go, so this appeared to me as a message from the Gods that my future definitely lay *en Afrique*.

I've always been quite brilliant at making life-changing decisions. This is because, despite my conviction that I have thought everything through and examined all the possible outcomes of my decision, I never in fact do anything of the kind. Move to Africa? Of course, no probs! The first thing to do was apply for my three-year volunteer visa which would do away with the necessity of returning to London every few months. So off I trotted to the SA Embassy, filled in the appropriate forms, handed over five hundred pounds and was told to collect my visa in ten days' time. Yippee!

I immediately booked my ticket to Johannesburg, thrilled that everything had worked out to the satisfaction of all concerned. I would make my home in Africa, and Vicki's mum could move into my self-contained flat as soon as Vicki had made it habitable for occupancy by said mum. I continued to stay with Vick while the flat was being converted; she was a brick and let me stay in her room whilst she moved into the spare room at the top of the house. This was profoundly noble of her as the bed in the spare room was only suitable for a child no older than seven and she didn't enjoy a good night's sleep for months. It should have been at the most three weeks, but then a rather large snag presented itself and my stay was extended for eleven months…

17
A Bird in the Hand…

Having been instructed by the Embassy to return ten days later to collect my visa, I was surprised after seven days to be telephoned by one of its staff informing me not to come as agreed but to wait for the letter I would shortly receive from them. When I finally retrieved the letter (which had been sent to the wrong address) I gave it to Vick and said, 'You open it; I'm convinced they've turned me down and I'm not sure I'm ready to deal with that.'

She opened it, read the contents, looked at me and said 'You're right, they have turned you down.'

I grabbed the offending piece of paper from her and read the letter which informed me I had been refused a visa on the grounds that I was 'a drugs trafficker'. As I had never sold a drug in my life and as my offence had been 'possession' I knew that a huge mistake had been made and sat down and wrote a letter to the Embassy pointing this out.

Eleven years previously I had travelled by plane to stay with the parents of Richard Hansell. His father who was then seventy-two years of age suffered acutely from arthritis, and having discovered that cannabis was a known pain-reliever for the condition asked if I could possibly bring him some over. I made a couple of phone calls, received the bounty, popped it into my handbag and made my way to Stansted airport where I was to catch a flight to somewhere in Scotland. Because it was a domestic flight I assumed it would be like getting on a train and was totally unprepared for the X-ray machine that greeted me as I arrived in the departure area. On went my handbag to be picked up as it exited from the machine by a very dour jobsworth who opened it, produced the Bob Hope from its obviously inadequate hiding place, held it up and enquired, 'And what, madam, is this?'

The game was definitely up so I said rather cheerily, 'That, darling, is cannabis resin.' He moved me to one side, called the airport police and informed me that I would be placed under arrest. I made that little fucker's day!

Two policemen arrived to take me to the airport cop shop and said if I promised not to run away, they wouldn't put handcuffs on me. Handcuffs! For heaven's sake, I was hardly a risk to security even if I did decide to leg it. They turned out to be huge *Blake's 7* fans and were tickled pink to have arrested Servalan.

At the cop shop, I was photographed and fingerprinted whilst a telephone call was made to the CPS. It appeared that the amount I was carrying was slightly over that deemed suitable for personal use and there was no alternative but to prosecute me. I was finding the whole experience rather jolly: it was the closest I'd ever got to appearing on *The Bill*. I was then put into a cell whilst phone calls were made and reports written up. After an hour or two, one of the arresting officers appeared, unlocked my cell, handed me a cup of tea, and asked if there was anything else he could get me. 'A joint?' I said, quick as a flash. My request was refused and he left the cell, locking the door securely behind him. I found his refusal rather irrational; they knew I was a smoker (I hadn't mentioned anything about Richard's father) and as I was imprisoned and guilty I thought a spliff to calm my nerves was only humane – an attitude not shared by the boys in blue.

I was then taken to an interview room to give my statement and we had the following conversation:

Officer: From where did you obtain this substance?
Me: From my friend Mo.
Officer: And where can we find your friend Mo?
Me: Why do you want to find Mo?
Officer: So we can arrest her for being a supplier.
Me: Don't be ridiculous, I'm not going to snitch on Mo. In no way is Mo a supplier; she doesn't even smoke herself, she got it from a friend who does.
Officer: And from whom did Mo obtain the substance?
Me: Her friend Marilyn.
Officer: And where can we locate Marilyn?

By this time I was thoroughly ensconced in my role of freedom fighter, and determined not to betray my comrades no matter how intense the interrogation became. I was finally returned to my cell exhausted but unbroken before being released an hour later.

The arresting officer told me that I would receive notification of my court appearance by post and assured me that my criminal record would be deleted from my file after a period of five years. It would never prevent me from obtaining a visa to visit America or indeed anywhere else. Wrong! So far I have been banned from two continents for life, one of them being America. Surely a lifelong ban for a minor offence committed over fifteen years ago is a touch heavy-handed? It appears that the law was changed after the Soham murders. A police check on the perpetrator showed him to have a clean sheet, but only because his previous offences had been deleted after the five-year period. If they had had information from prior to that period they would have discovered that he had committed offences towards children before, and in no way would he have got the job of caretaker at the local school had it been known. So now, any offence, no matter how trivial, stays on one's record for life. To make no distinction between murderers and sociopaths on the one hand and those who enjoy a spliff on the other is surely a tad over the top.

I had of course missed my flight and required a new ticket to enable me to finally get to Scotland. It was proving to be an expensive trip. But my arresting officer walked me over to the ticket counter and explained that I had missed my flight as I had been 'helping them with their enquiries'. He made it sound as though I had been a witness rather than the criminal and I was given a ticket free of charge which did cheer me up somewhat.

We said our goodbyes and just before he turned to leave, he looked at me and chuckled. 'You're a girl, you are,' he said, giving me the distinct impression that he'd thoroughly enjoyed the whole experience.

When I appeared in court some weeks later, I was fined fifty pounds for the offence and sixty pounds court costs. And that, I thought, was that.

So in my letter to the Embassy, I pointed out that drug traffickers usually carried more supplies than half an ounce of black; would choose somewhere more suitable to conceal them than in a handbag; and far from receiving a fifty-pound fine, as a trafficker I would doubtless still have been behind bars. My entreaties fell on deaf ears. I went to the Embassy to plead my case and asked if I could return to South Africa on a three-month visa while my case was being heard. 'You can never return to South Africa again,' was the response.

'But I've never sold a drug in my life!' was my impassioned reply. 'You have to let me back!' They weren't budging. They told me that it would take three months to review my case and if I made any attempt to travel to South Africa I would be arrested at Heathrow as they had been informed that I was not allowed to return. I was in bits.

I immediately telephoned Arthur from London to tell him of my plight. 'But they can't stop you from returning,' he said. 'This is your home!' Having been told at the Embassy that I should never have been at the sanctuary in the first place as I had been travelling on a visitor's visa as opposed to a volunteer's visa, I explained to him that the authorities wouldn't share his point of view. We continued to text and talk to each other during my exile.

After three months there was still no news and I began to haunt the Embassy: a hollow-eyed, distraught figure who was obviously barking and to be treated as such. I held myself together for five months before I finally cracked completely – big time. I went to see my doctor who immediately referred me to the Emergency Psychiatric Unit, aka 'the madhouse'. My antidepressants were increased but did no good at all; I was to continue to report there twice a week for treatment.

Two of my closest friends are the magnificent actor John Hurt and his equally magnificent wife Anwen. I had known John since my RADA days, done my first telly with him and bumped into him occasionally over the years, but our friendship only really began to evolve into our present one when we worked together in Africa on the film *White Mischief*. I was due to have dinner with them that evening, but as I was in bits and unable to stop crying I texted Anwen to say I would be unable to attend.

Five minutes later my phone rang. 'Darling, what is it?' asked John. I explained the situation and he said, 'Why don't you get yourself into a taxi and come over?'

'Because I can't stop crying Johnno, I'd be appalling company.' (I should make it clear that I am the only person alive allowed to call John, Johnno: a dispensation for which I'm extremely grateful.)

'Come over here and cry darling, I'll be outside waiting for you.' Such kindness. I went over and poured out the whole story.

There is no doubt in my mind that John and Anwen saved my sanity and probably my life, and in no way am I being dramatic when I make that statement. The despair that permeated my being was unsupportable. The demands it made on my body were impossible to sustain. I always emerged from these states considerably weakened and I was very aware that my body couldn't take much more. To finally find everything that I had searched for all my life at the late age of sixty-three, only to be told I was forbidden to live there was akin to reaching the gates of Paradise only to have them slam shut in my face. I knew I was losing my grip on what remained of my sanity, and was very aware that – if I didn't drop off my perch first – it was only a matter of time before men in little white coats appeared to take me away. I no longer had the will to live; who would in that situation? I had nothing, absolutely nothing to warrant staying alive; my life was an ongoing nightmare from which I had to escape.

John and Anwen walked that extra mile for me: did everything in their power to support my return to my beloved Africa, my monkeys, my dogs and my *home*. They refused to allow me to give in and insisted I keep up my constant visits to the Embassy. Every time I lost heart, they assured me I hadn't and to keep up the pressure. And how right they were; eventually I was told that my persistence had paid off and I was to get my visa. By then I think they were willing to do anything just to get rid of me. At any rate, it took a further six months but when I left the Embassy for the last time, eleven months after my arrival in England, I was clutching my three-year visa.

I no longer had a home in England; my relationship with Vick had been damaged by our 'divorce' and I had moved out of her house. Three weeks before I heard my visa was about to be granted I found myself without a roof over my head; I'd been staying with another friend but it was no longer convenient to have me there. John and Anwen immediately lent me their flat in central London. I have never asked J for money, but then I've never had to. He's popped folding money into my handbag on more than one occasion. He once took me to the Ivy for dinner and between the starter and the mains handed me an envelope. Inside were three thousand dollars which he said were his unused *per diem* on a recently completed film, together with a card saying 'non return'. Such class!

Another time when I joined them for dinner, Anwen suddenly disappeared into the kitchen and John and I had the following conversation:

J: Darling, we've been thinking, you've been in this country far longer than you anticipated, and London is vastly more expensive that Africa. Are you all right for money darling?
Me: Absolutely fine Johnno, couldn't be better.
J: You're sure about that Jacko?
Me: Really, Johnno, I'm absolutely fine.

(Long pause)

J: You would tell me if you weren't, wouldn't you Jacko?
Me: Of course darling. No worries.
J: It's just that I've a thousand pounds next door, and it's got your name on it.

(He leaves the room and returns with a grand in readies which he proceeds to flick back and forth in front of me. I look at them mesmerised, reach for my open handbag and say:)

Me: Put it there!

To give someone money and in no way trespass upon their pride is a rare skill. Both John and Anwen have that skill in spades. It is not in me to borrow money, but I love presents and feel it would be churlish not to accept them in the spirit in which they are given. I once borrowed a grand from a friend – it took me several years to pay it back but I eventually did – and it caused me so many sleepless nights that I vowed never to do it again.

The more mean-spirited among my acquaintances have been heard to mutter, 'Well, he's rich enough, he can afford to be generous.' Bollocks! Wealth is no guarantee of generosity. Alan Bates wasn't short of a bob or two, and I could never in all honesty say that he was noted for his ability to 'flash the cash'.

FROM BYFLEET TO THE BUSH

A couple of years prior to all this, I had been approached by a writer to appear in a play he had recently completed. After numerous script/cast changes and the search to find a theatre willing to accept it, it was finally due to go into rehearsal on January 2nd 2009. I had intended to return to London at the beginning of rehearsals, but finding myself still in exile that had proved unnecessary. Knowing I had this play to do was also an important factor in enabling me to continue putting one foot in front of the other.

With one exception – in my opinion – I was in a company of talented actors, two of them quite exceptional: Gary Amers and Jamie McLachlan. The majority of my scenes were with Gary and I loved every second of being on stage with him; although I'm not absolutely sure he felt the same way about me. (I say that with my tongue firmly in my cheek as I know for a fact that he loved living dangerously!) The script deviated between modern-day language and something rather esoteric and I found the esoteric language extremely difficult to learn, principally because I had no understanding of its meaning. Asking the writer to explain didn't provide a great deal of enlightenment as his explanations were also rather esoteric, which I found more confusing than clarifying; so I had great difficulty retaining lines I didn't understand. So Gary and I went on each night with our hearts in our mouths and our fingers crossed. When I finally managed to get all the lines out, I turned to Gary as we came off stage and said triumphantly, 'I did it Gary! I did it! I finally remembered all the lines!'

'You did darling,' he said, 'well done! If you can now manage to get them in the right order it would help enormously!'

Gary is one of my favourite people in the entire world: seriously talented, with the voice of an angel; a brilliant mimic, a stunning dancer and covered in charisma. He was very funny, impressively intelligent and a powerful spirit. Gary and I would laugh together to the point of hysteria; unable to catch our breath, rolling around on the carpet, legs waving in the air, tears streaming down our faces in paroxysms of mirth. We adored each other and when that boy receives his first Oscar I'm going to applaud more loudly than anybody.

By this time I had moved from Vicki's and into the spare room of our writer/director, Matthew. As the theatre we were playing and rehearsing in was the White Bear in Kennington, and as its front door was directly opposite Vick's front door and my new lodgings were a tube journey away, I found a certain poignancy in my new situation. Matthew was employed as a writer on *Hollyoaks*, received a very good salary and lived in some splendour in a very smart flat in the West End. Unable to find a backer for his play he decided to use thirty grand of his own money in order to get it performed; a considerable sum to produce from one's own pocket.

We were rehearsing certain scenes at Matthew's flat prior to commencing rehearsals at the White Bear. One day most of the cast had assembled there as we were called for a photo shoot. He'd gone out briefly and returned with a takeaway cappuccino. He was obviously having a wobbly because he suddenly turned on everyone and said, 'Don't expect me to buy you lot any coffee as well because I'm practically broke; you can take care of yourselves.' As no one had asked him to buy them a coffee this came a little out of left field.

The play was not a success; it had its only showing at the White Bear and seemed unlikely ever to see the light of day again. And Matthew had lost all his money. The producer that Matthew had hired neglected to inform the press of our opening night, so we played to lots of jolly and biased friends, who all enjoyed themselves enormously, but absolutely no one who could actually advance our cause and inform the general public that we existed. With only a three-week run, by the time word had got around and we were playing to full houses and members of the press began to straggle in, we were two nights away from our final performance.

We were a very happy company until Matthew succeeded in alienating me from the entire cast with the exception of

Gary and Jamie. As the run progressed, his hostility towards me increased; he would behave charmingly after a performance as he introduced me to anyone he thought might assist his huge ambition for a West End transfer, and then morph into a vicious queen when he hit the front door. He was unable to accept that his failure to achieve recognition as the creative genius he saw himself to be was the result of his own script failing to impress. He needed a scapegoat and I was it. He spread it around the company and the profession that my inability to retain his lines was because I was a desperate dopehead and always stoned. I was a liar, a scammer, a schemer and lacking in any kind of respect. Joel had been employed as a hairdresser for the photo shoot; I had recommended him to our producer when he was unable to locate one himself. And that was all I'd had to do with the situation. Matthew accused me of colluding with Joel to enable him to get the job and his fee.

His ability to alienate me from a company who had previously held me in high regard and great affection, and who knew the weakness of both his character and his writing, not only saddened but surprised me. I would have expected them to have given me more credit. Without the support of Gary and Jamie, I would have been completely isolated.

It should have come as no surprise to me that the combination of pressures – the severance of my relationship with Vicki, the loss of my home, my exile from Africa, my complete lack of finances, Matthew's hostility and the loss of company support – finally tipped the balance. One night towards the end of the run, I went into the bar after the performance and became aware that I was beginning to unravel at an alarming rate. I went back to the – mercifully – empty flat, locked myself in my room and howled my anguish and desolation to the four walls that surrounded me, before finally falling into a coma of exhaustion.

What I didn't discover until the following day was that Matthew's next-door neighbour, whose bedroom wall abutted my own, had heard my – I have to admit – inhuman cries and, convinced that a homosexual orgy was taking place and a young boy was being abused, had summoned the police to register their suspicions and place a very strong complaint. I immediately wrote a letter of profuse apology to his neighbour and explained that the noise he had heard was not made by a young, abused boy, but by an elderly woman who was engaged in the process of ridding herself of a considerable amount of stress. I followed this up with a visit and a large bouquet of flowers and was able to absolve Matthew of any involvement in the mayhem that I had unwittingly created. The police had threatened Matthew with an ASBO which I understand was not enforced.

After our final performance I attended the cast party, was one of the last to leave and returned to an empty flat around midnight comatose with exhaustion. I took a sleeping pill and surrendered myself to the merciful oblivion of sleep. I was awakened around two a.m. by Matthew who had arrived home with some friends, determined to continue partying until dawn at the very least. I explained that I was exhausted, had nothing left to offer and would provide very poor company.

'But it's the last night,' he protested.

'It is indeed, but I have given my final performance, attended the party and am now firing on very few cylinders, if indeed any at all. I have to sleep.'

He returned to his guests and complained vociferously about my 'lack of respect'. Gary – who was one of the guests – pointed out that I was sixty-five and entitled to be exhausted.

The following day Matthew left for wherever it is that *Hollyoaks* is filmed and made it absolutely clear that I was to be gone, with no trace of my occupancy remaining, by the time he returned in two days' time. I cleaned the flat, left him a card, a bottle of champagne and a bouquet of flowers, filled the fridge with his favourite foods and closed the door of his flat for the final time, believing that I had acquitted myself as honourably as I could and wended my way the short distance to John and Anwen's flat, where I was greeted by Anwen with warmth and reassurances and made to feel completely welcome. The three weeks I remained there until my visa was finally granted and I was able to leave for Africa allowed me to lick my wounds in total privacy (John and Anwen were at their home in the country) although I remained bruised and raw for some time to come. Thus ended my last experience as a thespian.

18
Bush Baby

Four weeks before I was finally granted my visa, I received a call from Dave. I knew immediately what he was going to tell me. Arthur had died suddenly of a heart attack. And my heart contracted with grief for the loss of this beautiful man. He was infuriating, intractable, wise, elegant, autocratic, aristocratic, insecure, intransigent, passionate, very, very lovable and totally *unique*! I will not meet his like again and the loss of my friend and companion was indeed a heavy blow.

With Arthur's death, his partner Dave and Dave's wife Josie assumed overall control of the sanctuary. They instigated many changes which included getting rid of the remaining long-termers. Lisa had already left to pursue her new challenge of working with physically and mentally disabled children; Lornie was about to return to England to study for a degree in primatology having decided to leave of her own accord before she got the boot; so that left Vicky, Ryan, Indy, Rudi and myself of the original group of seven (Dave having assured me during our phone call that he wanted me to return).

When I arrived at the sanctuary Vic and Ryan had been sacked and requested to leave as soon as possible. They had moved to a nearby bush pub and were still in shock from the loss of Arthur and their dismissal from their monkeys and their home. They were given their bus fare to Johannesburg and that was it. Indy was told she could remain, but when she returned to England on a sabbatical shortly afterward she received an email from Dave informing her that her services were no longer required and she was effectively fired. What appallingly shabby treatment of three young people who had worked for several years with the monkeys: whose devotion to them was total, had worked for no money and very little appreciation. The night I arrived back, Indy met me at the bus station and we immediately went to join Vic, Ryan and Lornie at the bush pub. They were inconsolable, so we consumed a great deal of alcohol and some excellent home-grown in what soon turned into a wake. We all understood Dave and Josie's desire for a clean sweep, to start afresh with their own ideas and staff, but their treatment of those kids – in my book – was cruel and inhumane. And I know they all suffered greatly for a long time after their return to England. Indy is now studying primatology in England, and Vic and Ryan have been asked to start their own sanctuary in another part of Africa. I admire them all so much for their ability in the face of their huge loss to continue with their lives in such a mature and positive way.

Almost six years have passed since I first set foot on African soil and without question they have been the most rich, eventful, vivid, dramatic, powerful and ecstatic years of my life! I've been thrown upon resources I didn't dream I possessed and survived by myself in the bush. I had to leave the sanctuary and move into a small house very close by with a fellow volunteer I privately thought of as Hitler ten minutes after we moved in. Since she left about fifteen months ago, I've lived alone. By that I mean I don't live with humans; but I do live with animals. Three dogs, the oldest of whom is Snooze – a bush special (as opposed to a pavement special had she been conceived in a town) but with a face that suggests Jack Russell and a body that screams Staffordshire bull terrier. She's enchantingly pretty with large eyes that dominate her face and which she uses to great effect. She moved in with me and followed me when I left the sanctuary, where she'd lived for the past eight to ten years; no one knows her exact age, but I think she's about twelve now.

Toska is a toy Pomeranian, whom Hitler bought from a neighbour and proceeded to neglect quite spectacularly once she'd acquired him, as had his previous owners. They had bought him and a lady friend for the sole purpose of breeding; but when one of their large dogs inadvertently stepped on the lady friend, snuffing the life out her, Toska was put outside to fend for himself. Pomeranians are totally unsuited to the African climate: they have coats that resemble sheep's fleeces and reach to the ground. They are extremely high maintenance and should not be undertaken lightly. When Hitler bought him he was already covered in fleas, his tail matted with piss and poo and he wasn't house-trained. She did nothing to relieve his discomfort or make him more socially acceptable. I de-ticked him and, when she returned to Canada for a visit, had his coat clipped very short and his tail completely shaved, which was the only way to rid it of the massive accumulation of waste and wildlife that had been harbouring in its interior for months. When she decided to return to Canada for good, she dumped Toska on me, refused to pay for any future vet bills and pissed off.

But I had no qualms about accepting Tossie and he's turned out to be worth a guinea a minute. He visits the beauty parlour every month and returns having been trimmed, shampooed and set and sporting one pink and one blue bow and a fluffy, powder-puff tail. His party trick is to sit on his hind legs and pedal furiously with his front paws. It's a winner every time. Being the result of appalling inbreeding he isn't really a proper dog: he was designed to be an accessory, and so far I've resisted my impulse to deck him out in a diamanté collar with matching earrings and a pink coat liberally sprinkled with sequins. When he first returned from the beauty parlour he had only the one blue bow; when I enquired why, I was informed that girls got two pink bows, and boys one blue one. 'He's gay,' I said, 'give him one of each.' We're both much happier now that he has two.

But I can't deny that he is like a toy: a teddy bear with boot-button eyes that follow my every move. He's the most expressive dog I've ever known and extremely demanding. If he feels that he's not the centre of attention, up go the front paws and he not only pedals vigorously but grins while he's doing so. I kid you not. He delights me and has me rocking with laughter on a daily basis. And Tossie is about five.

Rusty is a thoroughbred Jack Russell and a spectacular example of the breed. He's completely white except for his face, which is the colour of toffee with chestnut highlights and a perfect W shape joining the white of his body to the toffee colour at the nape of his neck. He was also covered with ticks and fleas with every rib showing when I asked the neighbour who owned him if I could have him – the same neighbour that Tossie came from. He now has a sturdy body with rippling muscles and glows with health. If I was a lady Jack Russell, his life wouldn't be his own. Rusty is about four so is also the youngest.

Living with my kids as I unashamedly call them is a joy, and apart from my forays into town once a week we are together 24/7. They are the family I never had and always wanted, and I wouldn't trade my canine kids for human offspring for all the diamonds *en Afrique*. I adore them and the feeling is entirely mutual. We delight in each other's company and get our greatest fulfilment from being together. Obviously we sleep together – under the duvet – and when I settle down at night doing spoons with Rusty who curls up next to my tummy, and feel the warmth of Snooze snoring against my back and Tossie who makes a nest in the pillows behind me, as far as I'm concerned life has nothing better to offer. It's from animals that I've received the unconditional love I've been searching for all my life; with animals that I know the joy of home and family – a joy that hasn't proved possible for me with human beings. Because with human beings, even in the most harmonious of relationships, there will always be the occasional discord, disappointment, emotional upheaval and the continual need for readjustment which seems to require constant compromise. Which is fine if that's what you want and consider acceptable because you feel that on balance the advantages outweigh the disadvantages. But I definitely don't! I want what I have with my kids: constant harmony, endless joy, and no fuckin' hassle! I can live a life of love; it's the only life I want to live, and the only way I've found I can achieve it is to hang out with animals. Obviously relationships with animals are far, far less complex than relationships with human beings but I revel in that simplicity.

When I say they're substitute children, I mean in the sense that they require my maternal skills in a similar way to children. They need to be fed and watered, exercised, played with and loved. Unlike children they are not required to attend school and be chauffeured around to ballet classes, brownies/scouts, piano lessons, footie practice or tea parties; nor do they require the seemingly endless tasks and vast expense involved in child-rearing. And like animals they need to be loved: first – last – and certainly foremost. I'm not convinced that all of us experience this parental devotion. What I am convinced by is that no woman should even contemplate having a child unless her desire for that child is her *raison d'être*. If you are a woman of huge talent and expertise and fired with ambition: go for it girl! But don't have a child as well. It simply isn't possible to serve two masters equally: your ambition and your responsibility for your child. It simply isn't possible to 'have it all', and enough women are drowning in a quagmire of guilt, exhaustion and regret to give veracity to my belief.

Before I continue any further in this vein, let me say that I'm fully expecting to be stoned by the Women's Liberation Movement but in no way deterred by the prospect. What I am expressing are my own conclusions based on my own experiences in life. I did not receive the irreplaceable gift of unconditional love. My mother was too immature, far too much of a child herself to undertake the awesome responsibility of motherhood; and I understand her situation totally and feel nothing but compassion for her. But the consequences of her abandonment rendered me emotionally crippled and in great pain for many years; pain which could have been avoided had I been in receipt of the unconditional love bequeathed from mother to child which I am convinced should be every child's birthright – but alas, rarely is.

My life is extremely simple and the simpler it becomes the happier I am. In the eyes of the world I'm a complete failure: sixty-eight years old, unmarried, childless, completely broke and unemployed; have made no contribution to the world and will leave it unnoticed except by some diehard sci-fi aficionados and some very close friends (for whom I'm eternally grateful); and living in a tiny rented property with very few possessions. But as I spend my days wafting around in a state that feels very like bliss, telling trees, animals and plants, 'I love you Africa, I love, love, love you. Thank you, thank you, thank you, I'm so happy, happy, *happy!*' you won't hear me complain.

I do understand that that description of how I spend my days is naff at best and probably vomit-making at worst, and can only apologise for the poor quality of the prose used to convey my present euphoria. It's a huge miracle! After a lifetime of pain and depression, to find myself free of it, to discover the 'me' that had been almost totally buried under the mountain of inherited shit that until now had swamped me, is I suggest akin to being reborn. We all live with inherited shit as our parents lived with theirs; it's part of the human condition and I can only feel compassion for all of us. And ultimately I consider myself to be one of the lucky ones. If our pain is not too great, we can deal with it: channel it into something constructive, or push it aside until the opportunity to free ourselves and become whole is no longer an option. Because I experienced my pain to a really inhuman degree, I had two able to explain what exactly it is about me that merits that description. And I'm not sure that I'm happy with it.

I posit that there are very few people on our planet who don't long – covertly or overtly – to be viewed as outstanding in some way; to stand out from the crowd, to be noticed and considered special. I'm all for that for myself, but the impression I get is that I don't fit into that category – which let's face it is exceedingly large. The nearest I came to a description of myself was some years ago when I said to a very close friend, 'Jo-Jo, I feel like a freak of nature.'

'You *are* a freak of nature, Jackson,' was her less than reassuring response, 'but you're also a gift from the Gods.'

However, in just what way I am a freak of nature, and also a gift from the Gods, I haven't even begun to comprehend. What I am certain of is that being *unique* ain't all it's cracked up to be. It is by definition a solitary path; and to be considered barking, which is many people's understanding of *unique*, is not always an easy row to hoe. Was I born this way; am I the result of nurture; or a combination of the two – or something that I haven't even considered because I have no idea what it is? Perhaps I am barking, but I have to say that as I'm having the time of my life, revelling in every second of it, does it really matter? I do no harm to man or beast, wish ill on no one (well, not very often and never for long) and am staggered by the amount of blessings I have to count on a daily basis. So I've decided to throw in the towel as far as a rational explanation is concerned and give my entire focus to celebrating the wonder of life as I now experience it. As great as my sadness was, so is the joy that now sings in my soul.

I continue to take antidepressants and achieve sleep with pills, but no longer consider that to be a failure on my part; as a diabetic is dependent upon insulin, so are many depressives reliant on chemical assistance. I've achieved my greatest desire, to be both loved and loving; am completely content with my little canine family, and eternally grateful for the peace and joy that now fulfil my life.

choices – life or death – and despite the fact that it took me many years, I gradually made my way like a blinkered donkey in a coal mine toward the unseen but intuited light which would eventually lead me to the integration I had been seeking. I'm the first to acknowledge that it's taken me a while; but far better very late than not at all.

I arrived in Africa at the age of sixty-two with a great amount of self-knowledge, but seemingly unable to fit the pieces together to make a complete picture of the jigsaw puzzle I felt myself to be. I still had depressions, though not as frequently; and the searing attacks of insecurity before they hit continued to torment me. There was an adult woman inside me as well as an insecure child but I was unable to merge them together; and, until I could, my inner child would never feel secure as inner mummy failed to materialise on cue. I would go along swimmingly until I was rejected: rejection being the trigger that floored me every time. By now I had the reactions of a Pavlovian dog and as soon as the trigger was pressed I submitted to grief and despair as I had done so many, many times before. It was like playing a record on repeat, and with each repetition I scored another track onto the vinyl until it was seriously close to burning out completely – and me along with it. The more aware I became of this pattern and process the more able I became to understand that that response was no longer necessary or appropriate. I was no longer an abandoned child but a woman in control of her own life. I had finally managed to merge the child with the mother and knew the luxury of security. This process was only finally completed in the past few months and is precious beyond price.

Throughout my life my image of myself has come from other people's reactions to me. The one I met with most frequently is that I appear to be completely outside other people's experience of human beings. I, apparently, am unique. 'But surely we're all unique,' I would argue. 'No, not like you're unique. You're *unique*.' And no one has ever been